Praise for Metal Spikes

As a manager and owner of a traveling baseball team, I believe Metal Spikes should be read by every single kid dreaming of playing baseball at a higher level... be it high school, college or professional. Not only does this book teach baseball fundamentals, it teaches "life fundamentals". The mentors in Billy's life are really mentors for all of us. I strongly recommend to all travel baseball managers to get this book for your players. It will help your kids become better ball players, and teach them how to dream big.

Sean Lewis
Manager and Owner
Buccaneer Traveling baseball
Houston, Texas

As an avid reader, I was impressed with the level of storytelling from a first-time author. Metal Spikes tells the story of Billy and his dream of becoming a professional baseball player. Along the way, the adults around him will show him what's important in the effort to realize that dream. The book shows a boy learning the power of paying attention to those adults and we hear the inner voice of an intelligent and driven individual as he makes progress toward that dream. I can't wait to read the other 6 books in the series and to see what happens to his friends as they work on their own dreams. A great book for kids of all ages and one that parents can use to teach life lessons in a fun and relevant way. It makes me wonder what I might have accomplished with these people around when I

was younger. Buy this for every child you care about and give them a fighting chance with their own dreams.
Bill Hagara
Austin-based Technology Entrepreneur

The target audience for this book is obviously young boys. But this older lady baseball fan loved it, too. It taught me a lot about the draft process and what goes on behind the scenes in the world of baseball. Can't wait to see what happens to Billy next. Great job by Mr. Haskin!
Catherine Athearn

The author of Metal Spikes covered all the bases". Failure/Success, Friendship/Hardship, Hope/Disappointment & oh yes, Sportsmanship. It definitely takes me back to Little League days & I think Metal Spikes is an outstanding read.
Jim Losher

The book Metal Spikes by Warren Haskin is a more than worthy read for any age interested is sports. A heartwarming tome .
William Harsh

Obviously, the author of Metal Spikes is someone who has lived the sport of baseball. For any kid dreaming of being the best baseball player ever, this is a great read. My guess is that the author was not only a ball player himself, but one of those guys that was the team spirit....a guy who doesn't give up, and is willing to work harder than anyone else. That's what this book is about. Every kid with that dream in baseball should read this

book. In fact, all kids should read Metal Spikes because it's about how to be successful in any field. I highly recommend Metal Spikes for kids and parents alike. This book is not only entertainment at its best, but educational for kids and parents alike.
RC Hines
San Diego, California

I am very excited to read the next book in the series of Metal Spikes. Amazing read - well done!
Commissioner Richard Pagliaro
Baseball Manager Leagues

"There is no way a young boy (or girl) can read Metal Spikes and not get something out of it that will improve his/her life. More specifically, if you are talented at a sport (or anything) and want to excel at it, you need to REALLY dedicate yourself. Getting a proper work ethic, as taught to Billy throughout the book, will help any kid excel at baseball or whatever he/she truly desires.
The Author makes a good case for all of us to get out of our comfort zone and apply ourselves to what we truly want in life. A new type of book for youngsters and parents alike".

Alex Hart
BBM Manager
George Brett League

3 & 2 count. Bases loaded. Bottom of the 7th. Billy dug in. He knew he was going to get a fastball. A single would tie the game. A HR would win the game and the national championship. The pitcher looked in to the catcher, got his sign, glanced over at the runner on third, and started his windup. Billy was ready. He swung.

RING!!! The alarm clock jolted Billy up and out of bed. His first thought was "did I hit it?" His second thought was, "today is the day."

Metal Spikes

Warren Haskin

Metal Spikes

Warren Haskin

Published By
Positive Imaging, LLC
bill@positive-imaging.com

ISBN 9781944071240

Contents

To my Dad, who built a baseball field for my Cub Scout Troop in the first "Field of Dreams" He knew I would love baseball all my life.

1

Real Baseball

With every step he took, the sound of the metal spikes hitting the parking lot surface thrilled Billy. He was beyond excited. It was finally time for his first real baseball game.

His Dad and Mom drove him to the field, where after a month of practicing three days a week, the KC Rockets were going to play their first Little League game.

He had been good at hitting off a tee, and when the coaches slow-pitched his team the next year. But this time, he was going to face a real pitcher with real baseball rules.

The nine-year old was fast, and he talked his Mom and Dad into getting him metal spikes so he could run faster. He thought "stealing a base" would be about the most exciting thing he could do.

He got out of the car, looking for his teammates. Bobby was over by the water fountain, and Coach Yam was sitting on the bench, looking over his lineup. Billy headed toward the water fountain, hearing the clang of his metal spikes hitting the pavement. That had to be the best sound he'd ever heard.

"Are you going to start?" Bobby asked. Bobby had been Billy's best friend since the 1st grade.

"I think both of us will start," replied Billy with excitement in his voice.

"Yeah, me too, "said Bobby, but Billy didn't hear him. He saw two of the Lions, who they were playing. They looked bigger and older than Billy. He stood there, watching them, and hoping one wasn't the starting pitcher for the Lions.

"Look at those guys, Bobby. Are they our age?" asked Billy.

"No way," replied Bobby. "Those guys have to be 11 or 12."

The two boys walked over to see Coach Yam to ask him if those guys were really who they were playing.

Before getting to the coach, one of the Lions looked over at Billy and said, "I didn't know they let rookies wear metal spikes," looking at Billy's brand new pair.

This was the first time he'd encountered razzing and didn't know what to say. He turned away and continued toward the bench.

Other team members arrived, and the coach assembled the team in the outfield. He emphasized that the Rockets were going to be a team, not just a bunch of kids. They were going to be positive when on the field or the bench. Negative attitudes would not be allowed, and he expected each kid to show appreciation to his fellow teammates when they did something good.

Billy and Bobby learned they both were going to start. Billy was starting at second base, and Bobby was starting at catcher. Billy was batting third, and Bobby was hitting cleanup. Then he got the bad news.

"Metal spikes are not allowed in this league, Billy. You will have to wear tennis shoes or plastic spikes", Coach Yam told him.

Billy's heart sank to the ground. He'd watched the World Series and thought "Jose Joslin was the coolest player on the team because he stole six bases." Now, Billy wasn't going to be able to steal any bases in those silly plastic spikes. He'd had to wear them last year when the coaches pitched, but this was real baseball, he thought.

He walked to his Dad to tell him, with tears in his eyes.

"Dad, Coach says metal spikes are not allowed in this league. I don't even want to play", cried Billy.

Jim Tankersly looked down at his son, put an arm around his shoulders and cried silently with Billy because he knew how much metal spikes meant to him. He finally spoke.

"Billy, as you grow up, you find out that sometimes things do not work out the way we want them to, no matter how much you want something. Remember our talk about visualizing what you want when you get up to the plate? Well, even then, if you get a hit one out of three times, you are considered a success. In other words, you are likely to make at least two outs, no matter how much you want to get a hit. The same is true in life as you grow up. You do not get everything you want", spoke Billy's Dad to him, "but you keep trying."

"But Dad, this is real baseball," yelled Billy. "Spikes should be allowed if us kids can play real baseball."

Jim Tankersly looked at his son, wanting more than anything to say something that would make Billy understand. He felt guilty because he should have checked with the league before buying the metal spikes for Billy. It was his fault that his son was heart-broken and there was nothing he could say other than giving Billy a pep talk, telling him that he could steal in this league, and was almost as fast in plastic spikes as he would be with metal ones.

That calmed him down a little, at least getting his mind back to the game ahead. Thankfully, he had a pair of plastic spikes in the car. As he changed, he was determined that he was going to get two hits, and steal two bases to show his Dad that just getting one hit was not considered successful....not in his mind.

Billy was excited when the umpire yelled, "Play Ball." He'd forgotten about his plastic spikes when he came up to bat. It was the big guy pitching, and he struck out Pepsi and Duke to start the game. Pepsi lived across the street from Billy and Duke a block over. They had played baseball in the neighborhood since they were just little kids, but none of them had seen a pitcher throw a pitch this fast.

Now it was Billy's turn to bat. He had been judging how fast the ball came in, standing in the on-deck circle. He stepped into the batter's box, looked at the giant, pitching for the Lions, and visualized hitting his fastball to the opposite field, a trick his coach last year taught him.

"Strike one," bellowed the ump after the first pitch.

Billy had never seen a ball thrown this fast, but he was determined to get the first hit for the Rockets. On the next pitch, Billy swung at another fastball and missed it.

"Strike two," yelled the ump.

With a 0-2 count, Billy faced a fear he'd never faced before. What if he struck out? Pepsi and Duke told him after they struck out that this pitcher was the best they had ever seen. He dug in, and made up his mind; he was going to get a hit. The next pitch was even faster than the first two. Billy swung. He knew he'd tipped it, but turned around hoping the catcher didn't hold on to it.

"Foul ball," roared the umpire.

On the next pitch, Billy swung and hit a sharp line drive to left field, just the way he'd been taught. The left fielder picked it up on one hop and threw to second base as Billy was rounding first base. A single. His first time playing "real baseball." "I love baseball," he smiled to himself.

Bobby batted behind Billy and was a good hitter, so Billy was a little surprised when he saw the third base coach give him the "steal sign" on the first pitch to Bobby. Billy looked at the pitcher as he took a lead. He didn't know how far he could get off the base since last year there was "no stealing." He did not want to get picked off, but "taking a lead" was something brand new to him. He stepped off about four feet, and all of a sudden, the pitcher threw to first. Billy dove back in and was thankful the ump said, "Safe."

Now, he knew a little more of what to look for if the pitcher was going to try to pick him off, so he took a five-foot lead and started running as soon as the pitcher's leg crossed the pitching mound. That meant he could not throw to first without it being a balk, so Billy was thankful for his Dad's advice about the rules of baseball. He slid into second base long before the ball was there. Billy had stolen his first base, in plastic spikes. It felt amazing.

2

Listen Intently

The game was not even close as the Rockets won 10-3. Billy had two more hits, driving in four runs and scoring two. But, he was most proud of the fact that he'd stolen three bases.

After the game, all the parents came up to him telling him "Great game, Billy." He smiled a lot that night getting a lot of "high fives" from his teammates. Coach Yam had the team gather in the outfield after the game, going over things about this game and telling them the next practice would be Thursday afternoon after school. About the only thing Billy remembered was Bobby coming up to him after the game telling him he definitely would make the major leagues. All Billy could think about was, "at least I could wear metal spikes" there.

On the drive home, Billy's Dad went through the game with him, almost batter by batter. He told Billy that he could have reached a ground ball hit to his left if he had just dived for the ball. He explained to be good in anything, you have to go all out, and getting dirty was what made a real baseball player.

Billy thought, "I am dirty from sliding." His Dad didn't stop there. He explained that when Billy struck out his second time at bat, he embarrassed himself and his team by throwing his bat down. That was not acceptable.

It was a short ride home, but Billy had learned even more than he had at the game. He decided that plastic spikes were "OK for now," but one day, he was going to lead the major leagues in steals, in metal spikes. Billy slept well that night, drifting off to sleep thinking about his first "at bat," and his line drive hit to left field. "That felt good," he said to himself before falling asleep.

School would not be out for two more weeks, so it was hard for Billy to concentrate on schoolwork with practice in four days. On Thursday, he had to take a test, and he failed it. The teacher even called his Mom to ask if her son was having some sort of a problem at home.

Julie Tankersly said, "No, not that I'm aware of. It's probably that his mind is on baseball."

Billy's Mom told his Dad, which Billy feared. What he feared was exactly what happened.

His Dad told him, "No baseball practice tonight, son. Your school work is more important than baseball, and if you cannot keep your grades up from now on, you cannot play on the team."

Billy went into a temper tantrum. He hit the wall, screaming at this Dad that it was not fair to keep him from playing baseball. He started crying. This had to be, "The worst thing to ever happen to him, even worse than having to wear the stupid plastic spikes," thought Billy. His Dad called the coach telling him Billy would not be to practice. He explained to Coach Yam the reason.

Friday was just awful at school because Billy knew he would not start in the game the next day since he'd missed practice. But, he also realized that he'd better listen intently to his teachers because from now on, he was going to get good grades.

The game started at 3:00 Saturday afternoon, and just as Billy suspected, he was not in the starting lineup. Noah Arome was starting at 2B. He wasn't nearly as good as Billy and batted 8th in the lineup. Billy sat at the end of the bench the first few innings, before sliding down to talk to Coach Yam before the 5th inning started. He asked if he was going to get to play.

Coach Yam looked down at him and said, "Billy, if you cannot keep your grades up, then you are not going to be able to play baseball."

Billy explained to the Coach that he knew that now and had paid attention to the teachers on Friday. He swore to Coach Yam that he would get good grades from now on.

The coach said, "OK, Billy. I will put you in next inning, but you cannot ever again miss practice because of bad grades."

Billy got a hit, his only time at the plate, stole second and scored a run in another victory for the Rockets. This time, they won 7-2, and after the game, the coach told them that they were good enough to win the league, but they had to practice a lot harder if they were going to do that.

Billy rode home with his Dad and Mom, listening to them talk about things that had happened in their lives during the day. There were no lectures about not diving for a ball or even discuss the game. Billy was disappointed that his Dad had not complimented him on his hit, even if it didn't come until the 6th inning. At least, he got in the game, got a hit and stole a base in his plastic spikes.

But, no one mentioned the game on the way home. Billy ate dinner, watched a baseball game on TV with his Dad, and in the second inning, his Dad finally said, "Nice hit, Billy."

That made him forget all about not starting. He was so proud. He'd made his Dad proud, and he realized that making your Dad proud was about the coolest thing a kid could do. He was once again, happy and fell asleep on the couch around the 8th inning. He remembered his Dad picking him up and putting him to bed, but even then, he was thinking about his stolen base and wondering why his Dad didn't compliment him on that.

School the next week was more interesting than he'd ever thought it could be. He had never been interested in "history" but the teacher....maybe just for him....explained the history of baseball. He learned that Abner Doubleday had, for many years, been known as the man who started baseball in 1839. But when historians had gathered all the facts, Mr. Doubleday was found never to have even visited Cooperstown, New York, where it was known to be the site of one of the first baseball games. The historians could not agree who the founder was, but some said it was a man by the name of Alexander Cartwright, who had written the first rules of the game in 1845 for a team in New York called the "Knickerbockers." The true origin may never be known, but supposedly, Mr. Cartwright headed to the west coast to discover gold, and along the way, he taught others how to play baseball using the rules he had written.

"Mr. Cartwright is in Baseball's Hall of Fame, but Abner Doubleday is not", said his teacher. Billy found history to be interesting if it was something that interested him. Even when his teacher started talking about other things in American history, Billy listened intently and found it to be interesting too.

The nine-year old studied hard all week until Thursday came. There had been no tests this week, but Billy knew he would have received an "A" if there had been.

Practice started right at 4:00 PM with the coach gathering the team together telling them that they were going to skip batting practice this week and focus on fielding. Billy was a little disappointed, but ever since his Dad told him to dive for the grounder, he felt much better when playing defense.

He almost hoped ground balls would come his way, until Coach Yam said, "The first thing we are going to work on is double plays."

Since Billy played second base (2B,) this meant he was going to be in the center of the action at this practice. He was excited until he took his first throw from the shortstop (SS.) He threw to first base, and the runner beat his throw by a mile, at least it looked that way to Billy.

Coach Yam came up to him and explained that when he took the throw from the SS, third base (3B) or the pitcher that he had to touch the base with his left foot and throw as soon as the ball hit his glove. The coach showed him how and Billy couldn't believe he threw the ball almost before it even got to his glove.

It was only then that Coach Yam told Billy he had played 2B in the minor leagues, and although he'd never made the majors, he'd learned a lot from other professional players and coaches. Billy was listening even more intently to his coach after hearing that. All the rest of the practice session, he practiced getting rid of the ball as soon as he caught it. By the end of practice, Billy had thrown two practice runners out on double plays, and the coach had complimented him on being a fast learner.

School Friday was a little harder to concentrate, but he kept remembering what the coach had said, "Billy, you learn very quickly." He knew it was because he had been listening intently to the coach at practice yesterday when explained how to make a double play, so he worked all day at paying close attention to what his teachers were saying. When the final bell rang, Billy was thankful it was Friday because it meant there was a game tomorrow. Hopefully, he would start again.

It seemed like forever, but it was finally game time. Billy was starting at 2B and hitting third again. The Rockets won the game, 8-3 and were tied for first place. Billy had two hits and two stolen bases. But on the way home, his Dad complimented him on his fielding. He dove for a ball way to his left, and it surprised him; he caught it and threw the runner out. But, that wasn't what his Dad was complimenting him about. It was the double play he turned in the third inning. The batter had hit a hard grounder to Carlos Garcia, the shortstop who threw to Billy covering the bag, and he remembered, "Hit the bag with your left foot, and throw the ball as soon as you receive it." He did exactly that, and the runner was out by a step. Billy's Dad said that was the best thing he did all game, even better than his two hits.

He started to ask what his Dad thought about his two stolen bases, but before he could ask...his Dad laughed and said, "Those two stolen bases were pretty good too." Billy felt great but thought he could have stolen another base if he'd had metal spikes.

3

Championship Game

The rest of the season passed fast. School was out, so he played baseball every chance he got. The kids in his neighborhood played in the street or down at Suzie Gunn's house because she had a big side yard. He even tried switch hitting because there was a fence was in left field. In one of the Rocket's practices, he tried hitting right-handed against a real pitcher, and not just the neighborhood kid, who wasn't very good. He hit one ball further than ever before, but that was the only time he even made contact.

The coach said to him, "Billy, I think you will be better off just hitting left-handed."

From that day on, Billy only hit left handed, and his hitting got better and better. There were very few games during the season where Billy did not get at least two hits, and he stole a base almost every time he got on.

The final game of the season was against the Rangers, who were tied with the Rockets for first place. All his family members came, and the grandstands were packed. It was the first time Billy had played to such a large crowd. It seemed everyone was yelling. He felt like this was the most exciting day in his life.

His first time up to the plate he singled, stole second and came home on Bobby's double. The Rockets led 1-0 before the Rangers even knew what happened, but in the third inning, they scored two runs to take the lead. Billy didn't get up in the third, and the Rockets trailed 2-1 going into the 4th inning. As he stepped into the batter's box, he dug his plastic spikes into the dirt, staring at the pitcher. Billy was confident he would get a hit, steal second and come around to tie the game up. But, he hit a sharp grounder to the second baseman who threw him out before Billy was halfway to first. No one else got on and going into the bottom of the 7th, the last inning, Billy was going to be batting 4th.

He hoped someone would get on base so he could drive them in to tie the game. Liam Snow batted first and hit a line drive that the center fielder could not catch. Liam didn't stop at second base, and it looked like he might be out at 3B but he slid in under the tag, and the tying run was on 3B with no outs. Pepsi struck out, and Duke hit a pop up to 2B. It was Billy's turn to be the hero and at least tie the game. He had three home runs (HR) during the season, so he was thinking, "If I can get ahold of one, I could win the game for us." The count went to 3 & 2.

Billy was expecting a fastball over the heart of the plate because no pitcher wanted to face Bobby, the next batter. Billy watched the pitcher closely. He followed the ball from the time it left the pitcher's hand. He swung as hard as he could.

"Strike three!" the ump bellowed out.

Billy stood at the plate, not believing what had just happened. The other team raced to the field, jumping in the air, congratulating each other for winning the championship.

On the way home, his Dad tried to talk about next year, but all Billy could think about was that one pitch. All he had to do was hit a single, so why did he try to hit a HR? He cried. He slammed his helmet into the seat. Immediately, his Dad stopped the car, told him to get out, and right along the side of the road, he spanked him. His first baseball season ended with a spanking.

The winter came; his Dad was a basketball fanatic, watching every game of his alma mater, the University of Kansas. They were always good and were expected to get to the Final Four. For Christmas, Billy got a new "Billy Martin" glove and broke it in by throwing baseballs against the garage door all winter, except when the snow kept the ball from bouncing back. All the while, his Dad was glued to watching KU games. March came, and it was "March Madness," which would decide the National Championship. The Jayhawks played in the final game but lost 76-71. Billy watched his Dad throw his KU hat down on the floor, yelling "No, no." He was just as upset as Billy had been the first time he struck out and threw his bat down.

For the first time ever, Billy heard his Dad swear. "We lost the national championship because of the damn officiating."

"Dad," Billy said. "You taught me never to swear, and here you are swearing."

His Dad immediately apologized, explaining, "You know what Billy when bad things happen, you can get upset for a little while, but the secret to life and baseball, is putting the bad behind and looking for the good. I'm sorry I swore, and that is not something you should do."

Billy realized that adults get just as upset when their team loses as a kid does. A day hadn't passed that he didn't remember striking out last season with the tying run on third in the championship game.

Now, he wondered if his Dad would go all year, thinking about the KU game.

Just then, Dad said", Guess what happens next week? Your baseball practice starts!"

Dad seemed just as excited about that as Billy was....and his Jayhawk team had just lost.

Billy was 10 years old now and was playing in the same age group league. The other kids didn't look quite as big to Billy. He'd grown two inches that year and had a stronger arm than last year because of throwing the ball against the garage door all winter. He was still playing for the Rockets, but several of the guys had moved on to the 11 and 12-year-old league. Billy was thankful that Bobby, Pepsi, and Duke were still going to be on the team. No one seemed to remember that he'd struck out last year to make the final out. Everyone was just excited that it was mid-April and they got to start baseball practice again. Billy put on his plastic spikes, dreaming of the day he'd have metal spikes.

4

Mr. Treehouse

The Rockets had a good year. Billy was doing well and was invited to play in the 11 and 12-year-old league, but his Dad and Coach Yam discouraged him.

"Billy," his Dad said, "I think you should be very proud that you've improved so much that the Cardinals want you to play for their team, but the Rockets need you to win the championship."

Coach Yam chimed in, "If I thought it would really help you, Billy, I'd tell you to go ahead and join the Cardinals, but you might not even be starting for them."

He thought he would start for the Cards, but what his Dad said made more sense to him. The Rockets needed him. Billy realized right then what it meant to be a team player, and there was no way he was going to let Pepsi, Duke, Bobby and the others down by leaving the team.

As the season progressed, Billy and the team got better and better. By the end of the season, the Rockets were in first place alone and won the league championship. No other team even compared to them. Billy and Bobby had a contest all year to see who was going to have the highest batting average and most steals. Bobby didn't have a chance in the steals because of Billy, once again, was able to steal a base, and sometimes two, almost every time he got on base.

The catchers in the 9 and 10-year-old league were not very good, and when Billy got on base, the coach almost always gave him the steal sign. Billy didn't like his plastic spikes, but he found out that he was fast, no matter what spikes he had on.

This year there were two divisions, so there was still one game left for the "world series" championship. The Rockets were going to play the Pirates at Ban Johnson Stadium. This was the first time Billy had played in a real stadium. All their games had been on fields with dirt infields. This time, they were going to be playing on grass. He could smell it as he crushed the blades of grass under his plastic spikes.

During the regular season, Bobby hit .475 compared to Billy's .450 batting average. Billy was determined to get more hits in the championship game than his friend.

"I'll bet you an ice cream cone that I get more hits today," challenged Billy.

"Oh, you are so on. I'm going to get a hit each time up", replied Bobby with a confident grin on his face.

It seemed the entire team believed they were going to beat the Pirates. Even before the game when Coach Yam gathered the team in the outfield he told the boys, "You kids are better than the Pirates, but you will have to play your best to beat them."

He had the team gather in a circle, put their hands together and all yell at once, "Rockets!"

Billy and Bobby watched the Pirates pitcher warming up. "He's not as fast as that giant kid we faced last year," Bobby said.

"Yeah, but did you see his curve ball," said Billy, thinking that he'd never seen a ball curve like that. He just hoped he got fastballs.

The top of the lineup was the same with Pepsi leading off and Duke batting second. Pepsi hit the first pitch, which got by the center fielder, and he ended up with a triple. The Rockets bench was going wild.

"Way to go, Pepsi!" they yelled and then started screaming to Duke, "You can hit this guy, Duke. He's not as good as the pitchers in our league."

Coach Yam called a timeout and walked over to the dugout. "Boys," he said, "we can cheer our own team, but I don't want to hear you yelling at their pitcher. They may do it in the major leagues, but it won't happen on my team. Do you understand?"

They all nodded their heads and started yelling even louder for Duke to get a hit as the coach walked back to his third base coaching box. Duke delivered with a sharp single to left, scoring Pepsi. The Rockets were off to a 1-0 lead after only two batters. The kids on the bench were going wild, screaming at the top of their lungs.

Billy came up confident he could hit a homer off this pitcher.

He heard the bench yelling for him. "You can do it, Billy. You can hit a HR off this guy."

Billy thought the coach would stop the game again as the team was razzing the pitcher but he swung at the first pitch. The ball had to be the longest he'd ever hit. He watched it clear the centerfield fence.

As he crossed the plate, Bobby did a chest bump with Billy like they'd seen the Royals do. All the team came out of the dugout cheering. It definitely took his mind off striking out with the tying run on third last year.

The Rockets scorched the Pirates, 12-2. Billy and Bobby both had three hits, and Billy stole three bases. After the game, Coach Yam had the normal "after game" meeting in the outfield, and after everyone had quit celebrating, the Coach spoke.

"You kids played great all season long. You played as a team. You learned fast, all of you. Some of you will be joining the Cardinals next year, and I know you'll do well. But, I'd like to end the season with one last lesson. Most of you don't know this, but Billy was offered a chance to play with the Cards earlier this year and turned it down because he felt it would be letting all of you down if he left the team. That is what a "team" is all about and Billy, I want to thank you for putting the team ahead of yourself. That is what I'll remember about this season. You kids were a real team, and you all should be very proud. Have a good rest of the summer, boys and keep your grades up", the Coach concluded.

Billy was embarrassed because the Coach had singled him out but realized that teamwork was far more important than any individual statistic. Other members of the team came up and thanked him, which made him even more embarrassed.

"Hey Billy," he heard from the parking lot. "Come over here." He did not recognize the voice, so he didn't know if he should respond or not. Then he saw his Dad standing next to the man yelling to him. He walked over, hearing his stupid plastic spikes hit the pavement. He didn't know what his Dad and this stranger had to say, but he knew, he could hardly wait to play in a league with metal spikes.

"Billy, this is Mr. Treehouse, a scout for the Kansas City Royals", said his Dad.

"Why would a scout want to talk to me?" thought Billy. "I'm only 10 years old."

Mr. Treehouse explained that the Royals started looking for young boys who can throw and hit with power, along with having speed.

"Billy," Mr. Treehouse continued. "I've been scouting for years. I get to see many kids your age, up to college age, in looking for someone who might have enough talent to be someday signed by the Royals. Sometimes, we sign kids when they are 16 or 17, so that is a long time from now for you but I just wanted to encourage you to keep practicing hard and improving each year."

Billy was in seventh heaven. Not only had the Rockets won the championship but now a scout for his favorite team, the Royals, told him that if he kept improving he had a chance to play for the Royals when he was older.

On the way home his Dad said, "Billy, congratulations on winning the championship. You had a lot to do with the Rockets winning, and you should be a proud young man for putting the team ahead of yourself. Regarding Mr. Treehouse, I want you to understand. Tom is a friend of mine, who I invited to come to the game. He is a scout for the Royals but usually, does not start talking to a young boy until he's at least 15 or 16. During the game, he kept telling me, your son has power, speed, a good arm, and is very athletic. If he keeps improving, some day he might be someone we'd be interested in, so let me talk to him, and encourage him to keep improving."

Billy was bursting with pride, even if it was a friend of his Dad's.

But his Dad continued, "Tom told me that one thing lacking was you not being able to hit a curve ball and if nothing else, you needed to work on that next year. I'm going to spend time with you in the back yard, throwing you nothing but curves because I saw the same thing as Tom. You missed three curveballs and got all your hits on fastballs."

Billy realized that his Dad and Mr. Treehouse were right. He just was not able to hit the balls that curved. Not many pitchers in the 9-10-year-old league could even throw a curve or a changeup, but the ones who did had Billy's number. He remembered all year that he'd only hit one curveball and that was almost by accident.

"Dad," Billy asked. "Can we start tomorrow?" Mr. Tankersly smiled and nodded his head. Billy felt he was the luckiest kid in the world.

The very next day, his Dad woke him at 6:00 AM.

Billy was still asleep, but here was his Dad saying, "Come on Billy and let's see if you can hit a curve. I've only got an hour before I have to get ready for work, so from now on, you are going to have to be up and ready by 6:00 AM."

This was not what Billy had expected. "Does the sun even come up by 6:00 AM?" he thought. But if it took getting up earlier than normal, for him to learn how to hit a curveball, it was worth the price.

Dad had played catch with Billy many times. He hit grounders to teach him how to field better, but Billy had no idea his Dad could throw a curve until the first pitch came in. Billy swung and missed by a mile.

His Dad had built a backstop last year, so after 10 pitches, he would have to gather up the balls and throw them back to his Dad.

"Son," his Dad said, "Your head was looking over at the garage on each of those pitches, not at the ball when you swung. You need to watch that ball leave the pitcher's hand, but you also need to recognize the spin on the ball. To do that, you have to follow the ball until it hits your bat."

The rest of the hour they had together, Billy never once hit his Dad's curveball. Each time, he'd focus on the ball hitting the bat, but it would curve or drop at the last minute, and his bat would be far above the ball. With each miss, he got more and more frustrated, and when his Dad said that was enough for today, Billy was thankful. But he also knew that he was seeing the ball better at the end of the session than he had at first.

"Dad, where did you learn to throw a curve like that?" Billy asked.

When I pitched in the 3&2 League way back when, I learned to throw a curve, although I think it's better now", answered Mr. Tankersly, sort of amazed that his curve broke that much.

For the next 25 days, before it got too cold for his Dad, Billy practiced hitting a curveball. He was getting better and once, he actually saw the ball hit the bat. But each day as he put his plastic spikes on to take batting practice with his Dad, Billy dreamed of the day he'd be able to play with metal spikes.

Thanksgiving came and went. The same with Christmas, New Year's and then his 11th birthday. Billy knew it was getting close to Spring Training for the major leagues and that meant, he'd be practicing with the Cardinals soon. His Dad had not brought up their batting practice routine, mainly because he was so involved in his KU Jayhawk basketball team. The

Jayhawks were in the "Big Dance" again for the 26th straight year; a new college basketball record. They were projected to "win it all," according to what Billy read on the Internet. But sometime around the middle of March, the Jayhawks lost a game and their season was over.

The day after, Billy's Dad said, "OK, let's see if you can hit a curve." Billy was surprised that he was able to hit most of his Dad's curves. All the practice with his Dad last fall had helped him see the ball better. He was ready for baseball to start.

5

Change Positions

The Cardinals played in the 11 and 12-year-old league. Billy's birthday was on January 2nd, so he was one of the youngest in the league.

The kids looked a little bigger, just like him. Pepsi, Duke, and Bobby also were trying out for the Cardinals, and Billy felt at ease even though there were a bunch of new kids. The coach, Coach VanMussen explained to all of the kids that some would not make the team. He explained this was a tryout to see who could make the team and that would be announced after their fifth practice.

Pepsi came up to Billy asking, "Do you think I can make this team?" Billy, running toward the pitcher's mound where the coach was gathering all the kids, replied, "Sure, Pepsi."

The first practice was about hitting. Coach Van would pitch and see how well the players could hit. He threw mostly fastballs but would sneak in a curve to everyone during their at bat. Billy hit the first curve over the right fielder's head. Then Coach Van threw him another curve and Billy hit a line drive over 2B. All the coach threw him after that were fastballs but Billy felt good when his turn was over.

The next practice was fielding, and Billy drew compliments with the way he turned the double play.

Coach Van yelled, "Great arm, Billy!" after the last one.

Billy learned a big lesson at that day's practice as Coach Van had runners trying to break up the double play. Twice, the runner slid into Billy and prevented him from throwing the ball. It didn't take long for Billy to realize that not only did he need to tag the base with his left foot while throwing, he also needed to take a step back to avoid the runner barreling down on him. When practice was over, Billy thought he'd done better than the other kid trying out for 2B. He thought it was a sure bet that he'd make the team.

At the third practice, Coach Van told the boys, "Today I am going to time you as you run to first, and then to third base."

Coach Van never told any of the boys what their time was, but Billy was sure he'd been the fastest to first and to third even in his plastic spikes, which they had to wear again in this league.

When the practice was over, the coach called Billy over, "You may be the most athletic boy on the team. I'd like for you to try out as a shortstop."

"What," thought Billy? After playing two years at 2B and learning how to make a double play from that side, why did the coach want him to change positions?

"A shortstop is the most athletic position on a team, Billy," the coach started. "I think you'd help the team a lot more if we switched you to shortstop."

Billy didn't quite know what to think but if it would help the team and assured him a starting position, why not? He told his Dad when he got home from practice, and his Dad seemed to be happy for him, so Billy Googled, "how to play SS.". He learned that playing SS could be really fun. After watching about ten videos on YouTube, he got excited about the next practice.

Practice day came, and Billy learned how to make a double play from the other side of the diamond. He started feeling really comfortable on that side and was ready for games to start. They also hit during this practice and once again, Billy hit two curves the Coach threw him. After that, he saw nothing but fastballs. He hit the ball as far, or further than he ever had. He was glad his Dad built an exercise room for him during the winter. He worked out every day and felt like he was getting stronger.

After the last practice, Coach Van announced who made the team and who didn't. Billy wasn't too worried, but when he learned that Pepsi had not made the team, he was heart-broken. Pepsi was crying, and Billy didn't know what to say or do.

Billy remembered something his Dad told him two years ago and said to Pepsi, "Never quit. OK, you didn't make the team this year, but we'll still be playing together at Suzie's, and we'll work out together so you can make the team next year….just don't quit, Pepsi."

When he got home, he told his Dad what had happened, and it didn't seem to shock him at all.

"Pepsi is a very nice boy, but he lacks some of the skills needed. Remember what Mr. Treehouse told you. There are different things coaches or scouts look for. They look for overall athleticism, power, ability to make contact, speed and arm strength. Unfortunately, Pepsi is just not athletic", his Dad finished. Billy nodded "yes" to his Dad but went to sleep that night thinking about Pepsi.

The first game of the new season began with Billy starting for the Cardinals at shortstop. But instead of batting third as he liked, he was leading off.

Coach Van explained to Billy before the game, "I'm going to bat you lead off because I'm expecting you to get on base more than others on the team." He put his arm around Billy and continued, "You are the fastest on the team, and we will be doing a lot of stealing, but understand, the catchers are better here than you've ever seen. If you get thrown out, I don't want you to be discouraged."

Billy looked up at the coach thinking, "If I had metal spikes, I'd never get thrown out," but he didn't say anything.

The game started with Billy drawing a walk his first time up. He promptly stole second but was stranded there when no one else got a hit. His second time up, Billy looked down to third base to get Coach Van's signal and thought it was the sign to bunt. He wasn't sure, so he called timeout and walked down to Coach Van.

"Coach, was that a bunt sign?" he asked.

Turning them both away from the field so nobody could hear him the coach said, "Yes, I want you to bunt."

Billy thought, "I've never bunted in a game, but as he walked back to the plate, he was confident he could do it. He immediately popped the ball up to the pitcher and was out. He knew right then what he had to work on with his Dad each morning, who was still getting up earlier than normal to teach Billy different things about baseball. For some reason, they'd never practiced bunting.

The game ended with the Cardinals losing 5-4. Billy did not get a hit and struck out once on a fastball because he was expecting the pitcher, who was one of the best he had seen, to throw him a curve. He started to throw the bat down but remembered his lesson from year one. He walked back to the dugout, not wanting to look at anyone.

His teammates said, "Next time, Billy" but it was the 6th inning, and he would not get up again. After the game, Coach Van had a meeting in the outfield, the same as Coach Yam had done. Only this was different. Instead of praise, Coach Van told them he was really disappointed because they were better than the other team. For the first time since he'd been playing, it was the Coach who told him what he'd done wrong and not his Dad.

"Billy, there was a ground ball hit to your right. You picked it up the correct way, but you did not throw to first. Why?"

Billy explained he thought the runner was already there. The coach said, "No, he wasn't....if you'd thrown the ball, you would have gotten him."

Billy learned another lesson. It took more than "going all out" like his Dad preached; it was necessary to take risks. Coach Van explained to him that there were times in life you had to take a chance, even if you think you don't have a chance. Billy listened and learned.

The next game was against the Colts, and everyone knew they probably had the best team in the league, mainly because they were older and had played together for the past two years.

Before the game started, Coach Van told the players, "These guys are good, but you are better if you play your best. They can hit, so you are going to have to play great defense."

Billy led off by hitting a high fly ball to right field. He thought he had a HR but the right fielder caught up with the ball and made an unbelievable catch, at least in Billy's mind.

Out in the field, the Cardinals made some good plays themselves. Billy had a ground ball hit to his right, he backhanded it, twisted in the air and threw to first, not really expecting to get the runner. He threw it so hard and fast that the runner didn't stand a chance. Billy heard the coach yell, "Way to go, Billy."

From that point on, Billy felt right at home at his new position. After seven innings, the Cardinals had their first win. Billy had two hits and scored the winning run after stealing second. Bobby, who was batting third, singled up the middle and scored Billy easily. The score was 5-4, and the Cardinals jumped up and down, cheering wildly running toward Billy as soon as he crossed the plate. He was having so much fun; he almost forgot that he was still wearing those "stupid plastic spikes."

6

Better Not Criticize

With each game, Billy felt he was getting better, but something kept bothering him. Pepsi had stopped coming to their pickup games at Susie's, and that made Billy feel sad. One day when the kids were talking about going down to Susie's, Billy knocked on Pepsi's door to encourage him to come play.

"Hey, Billy. What's up?" asked Pepsi.

Billy told him they were going to start a game at Susie's and Billy wanted him to come to be on his team.

"Naw, I don't think so," said Pepsi. "I'm playing this video game, and I am really getting good."

Billy just didn't understand how a video game could be better than playing baseball, but Pepsi seemed happy, so Billy said, "OK, but if you change your mind, I want you on my team. Also, Pepsi, come out to some of our games. I miss you", concluded Billy, as he headed to Susie's.

The pickup games were only to occupy Billy's time when there wasn't a real practice or game, but in each game, he would try to get better. Susie came out to play with the boys on this day, and Billy realized she was as good as many of the boys.

"Why don't you come out for our team next year, Susie?" he asked.

"Girls don't get to play on boy's baseball teams, silly," she frowned.

"Who says?" quipped Billy.

"Have you ever seen a girl on any of the teams, Billy?" she asked, knowing his answer before asking the question.

He remembered something his Dad had told him last year. "Sometimes, Billy, life just isn't fair."

"This is definitely one of those cases," Billy thought.

But he had real practice the next day and forgot about everything except getting better. In batting practice, he got to take 10 swings. He was learning to wait for his pitch, which some of the kids had not learned.

Out of his 10 swings, eight would have been base hits in a game, and the coach said, "Nice job, Billy."

Billy gave a high five to Bobby as his friend approached the plate, and said, "Match that, fat boy."

It was like a nuclear bomb had hit. The coach stopped the practice immediately and almost ran to Billy.

"What did you say to Bobby?" the coach yelled. "I was just teasing him, Coach," said Billy.

"You should have learned by now," said the coach in a raised voice. "As a team, we encourage our teammates, Billy, we don't put them down, even if we are teasing. I want you to run laps around the outfield until Bobby gets done hitting."

With each step as he ran, he thought about what the coach had said. The kids teased each other at school all the time, "Why was this such a big deal," he thought. Then he remembered what Coach Yam told the team the first year, "There will be no criticizing, complaining or condemning on our team."

Billy realized that even though he was kidding, Bobby was a little husky and he'd probably hurt his feelings. Just then, as he rounded left field, Bobby hit a line drive that almost hit Billy because it was hit so hard. Billy laughed and said out loud, "Bobby may be heavy but he still hits better than me."

When Bobby had finished hitting, Billy apologized and said, "Bobby, I was just teasing you because you are a better hitter than me."

Bobby just shrugged his shoulders and said, "I know."

From that point on, Billy made up his mind that he would never be critical of anyone because of their appearance.

With only five games remaining, the Cardinals were in first place. Bobby was becoming known as the best hitter in the league and Billy was the best base stealer. Billy knew that Bobby's Dad had built a batting practice area, with a live pitching machine for his son and it was paying off.

"Hey Bobby," Billy called out after practice one day. "Would your Dad let me practice on the pitching machine with you?"

Without hesitating, Bobby said, "Sure, but you'll never be as good a hitter as me."

Billy thought back to his "fat boy" remark and wondered if this was the same, but ignored it, just being happy to get to use the pitching machine. The next day, he knocked on Bobby's door to ask him if now would be a good time for them to practice. Bobby's Mom answered the door and told Billy that Bobby had gotten real sick the night before.

"I'm getting ready to take him to the doctor's office to see if we can get some medicine, or find out what's wrong," she told Billy.

Billy walked over to Pepsi's to see if he was still playing his video games. Sure enough, he was. He asked Billy if he'd like to come in and play a game with him.

"I'm not very good at video games, Pepsi," said Billy, but he lit up when Pepsi told him he had a video baseball game.

"Really?" asked Billy.

When they walked inside, Billy realized that Pepsi had been playing this baseball game against the computer, trying to learn how to be a better player.

"How cool, Pepsi, let me see if I can beat you?" asked Billy. After two hours of playing game after game, Pepsi won each time.

"You are good, Pepsi," admitted Billy. "You definitely need to come out for the team next year. In fact, you should start coming to the games and watch what each of us does", encouraged Billy. "You might even come watch our practices, and I'll bet the coach would let you hit every now and then."

Pepsi shook his head, "No" and said, "Billy, let's face it. I'm not as good as you. Heck, even Susie is better. I know that, but I have fun on my video game dreaming that someday I can play again."

Billy didn't understand, but Pepsi seemed happy, so he told Pepsi "good-bye" and headed home for dinner.

"Dad, I stopped over at Pepsi's today, and he had a baseball video game," said Billy over dinner. "I think I know what I want for Christmas," mused Billy. He was thinking, "During the winter when I can't play; I could be playing the video game. I could even go over to Pepsi's to learn from him."

His Dad said, "We'll see," and the subject was dropped, but not in Billy's mind. He wanted to do anything to become a better player.

Bobby missed the next game because he had something called measles. Billy couldn't even go see him because it was contagious, so when the game started, the coach had the team pray for Bobby. That was the first time he'd ever prayed or been around someone who prayed since his family did not go to church. He wasn't quite sure what it all meant, but it felt good to have the entire team thinking of Bobby.

Duke ran over to Billy before the game started. "Did you hear?" asked Duke.

"Hear what?" asked Bill.

Duke sputtered, "About the new kid who might join our team."

"What new kid?" Billy asked, surprised.

"He's supposed to be super good. He just moved here from Mexico City", answered Duke.

Billy pondered this new information. "But, Coach Van didn't say anything about it," thought Billy out loud.

The game started before Duke and Billy could talk any more about a new kid, and as usual, Billy was studying everything that took place in the game. He studied the pitcher, the way the outfield played each batter, the way the coach on the other team gave signs.

There was nothing about baseball that wasn't thrilling to Billy. He was now starting to guess what type of pitch the pitcher would throw him. It was almost like he knew when the pitcher was going to throw a fastball or a curve. His hitting showed how much he was learning. For the first time all year, his batting average inched ahead of Bobby's with his three hits in this game. Of course, Bobby didn't get to play, but Billy felt good anyway after the team won 13 to 5.

On the way home, Billy asked his Dad, "Have you heard about the kid from Mexico City that is going to play on the team?"

His Dad searched for an answer. "I know a man and wife are moving here from Mexico City, Billy, but don't know much about them. I didn't even know they had a son."

7

Video Baseball

Bobby was past the contagious part of measles, so Billy went over to his house Friday to see how he was doing. He brought a couple of comic books for Bobby because he knew Bobby loved comics. Bobby looked at them and said, "Billy, you know I don't like "Spiderman."

Bobby's Mom spoke up, "Bobby that was not nice. You apologize to Billy immediately. He was trying to do something nice for you."

Bobby hugged Billy, telling him he was sorry.

"Hey Bobby, have you heard about this kid from Mexico, who might join our team?" Billy asked.

"What?" responded Bobby.

"Duke told me, but I don't know anything else," said Billy. "Maybe we'll find out more at the game tomorrow."

When Billy woke up Saturday morning, it was raining hard.

"Oh no," thought Billy. "The game might get rained out."

Just then the phone rang. It was Johnny Sanders, the first baseman on the team.

"Billy, Coach just called and said, "No game" today.

"He asked me to call you and wanted me to ask you to call Bobby, Duke, and Alex," said Johnny.

"Sure," said Billy, disappointed that the game had been called off. Billy called the others, and each responded the same as Billy, with disappointment.

"Do we get to have a make-up game, Billy?" asked Alex. "I don't know, Alex, but I have to think that if the race is close at the end of the season, we will have to make it up," said Billy, thinking again out loud.

He realized he did that a lot, without thinking what he was saying.

After hanging up, he called Pepsi. "Hey Pepsi, could Johnny and Bobby and I come over to have a tournament on your baseball video since our game has been rained out today?"

After Pepsi asked his Mother and she said "Yes," Billy called Johnny and Bobby.

Bobby's Mom said, "I think Bobby needs to stay indoors today in this wet weather to make sure he's over this sickness."

Billy texted Alex, one of the other kids who had an iPhone. "Can you come over to Pepsi's to play a video baseball game?"

Alex texted back, and 15 minutes later, they were all running through the rain to Pepsi's.

Since there was only one game, the four kids decided to play rock, paper, scissors to see who would play first. Billy knew that he did not want to have to play Pepsi. Sure enough, Alex and Johnny won, which meant they would play each other in the first game. Billy and Pepsi would play the second game. The winner of each would play each other for the "world series."

"Come on Alex, that's not fair," complained Johnny as Alex kept throwing the ball around the infield before he would pitch to Johnny. Finally, he pitched, and Johnny's batter swung and missed.

"How did you throw a ball that broke in and then out?" whined Johnny.

"Tricks of the trade," smiled Alex. In truth, he had no idea since he'd never played the game before. After three innings, the length they all had decided on before starting, Alex led Johnny 21-10. It was now Billy's turn to play Pepsi. Like in everything else, Billy wanted badly to win. He applied all that he'd learned the first day over at Pepsi's playing, and yet, Pepsi beat him 10-5. Naturally, in the "world series" game, Alex had no chance against Pepsi, and the final score was 18-3. No young boy could have been prouder than Pepsi that day.

It rained for two straight days, and the coach called off Tuesday's practice. Finally, on Friday, the sun came out and the field dried enough to take batting practice. Sure enough, there was a new kid at practice. Coach Van called everyone over to meet the new kid. His name was Miguel Angel Gonzales, and he didn't look big enough to play on the Cardinals, but when he took hitting practice, he hit the ball further than anyone else.

"What position do you play, Miguel?" quizzed Billy.

Miguel answered, but Billy had a hard time understanding his answer. Miguel saw that and said, "Me no speak good English."

Billy laughed and said, "Me no speak good Spanish either."

Both boys laughed, and at once, they knew they would be friends. Miquel was a good hitter, had speed and played centerfield. That meant that Sam might lose his starting position but the next day when game time came, Miquel was sitting on the bench and Sam was in his normal center field.

"OK boys, win the rest of your games and we will clinch the pennant," said Coach Van, trying to motivate the boys to play another good game. They did not disappoint him, and Duke led the way with two HR's in a 9-6 win. Billy was amazed at Duke's homers. Each time Billy tried to hit a HR, he'd strike out or at least miss the pitch. This was the worst game Billy had played since starting baseball. He had two errors, did not get on base once and on the ride home with his Dad and Mom, they kept telling him to not get down on himself.

He tried to think of other things, but all he could think of was his bad throw and missing an easy grounder. The fact that he struck out three times was just unacceptable.

"Dad, what was I doing wrong?" he asked.

"You were trying too hard," answered his Dad. "Why?"

"I don't know? Maybe because I wanted to show Miguel that I was the best on the team", answered Billy.

"Pride will get you no place," stated his Dad. "When you get prideful and think you are the best; that is when you will get taken down, Billy."

"I am the best," said Billy.

"Well, you sure were not today, Billy," said his Dad, in a scolding manner.

"Remember how you learned teamwork last year; remember how you didn't join the Cardinals the second year because you didn't want to hurt the team?" his Dad reminded him.

Billy was quiet the rest of the way home, but he thought about what his Dad had said. He vowed never to forget that valuable lesson.

That was the last game of the season he went without a hit. From then on, he showed Miguel and everyone else that he was the best by hitting over .500 and stealing 5 bases.

The Cardinals ended up winning the pennant again, and now it was time to play the last game of the year against the Razorbacks, a team in the other division which had not lost all year. They were in the West division, so the two teams had not played each other all year.

All the boys were excited to play an undefeated team in the other division; maybe a little thankful the Razorbacks were not in their division. They were going to play at Ban Johnson Stadium again, and that was exciting to all the boys.

Billy was still leading off, but Miguel was now batting second as he had beaten out Sam for the starting centerfielder's position. Bobby was batting third, and Johnny was hitting cleanup, the way it had been the last two games. Alex batted 5th, which meant he'd moved up two spots in the batting order since the first of the year. Billy wished he could be back hitting third, but by leading off, he did get to steal a lot more.

The Cardinals were the home team, so the Razorbacks batted first. On the first pitch, a hard ground ball was hit up the middle, but somehow, someway, Billy fielded it right behind second base, twirled around and threw a perfect strike to Johnny.

"He's out," the ump signaled.

The Cardinal fans roared their approval. The next two batters hit lazy fly balls to Miguel in center field, who made the plays look easy because he was so fast.

Billy came up to bat, thinking he was going to get a fastball to start the game. He was ready. The ball he hit went sailing over the pitcher's head so fast that he didn't have time even to raise his glove. Now Billy was on first, and he knew the steal signal was coming. But it didn't. On the first pitch, Miguel hit a line drive into the left-field corner, and Billy ended up on third with Miquel on second. Now, it was Bobby's turn.

Billy was thinking, "If the Coach had Miquel take a pitch, I could have stolen second and scored the first run by now."

Bobby took that thought away on the first pitch, hitting the ball 50 feet over the left field fence for his 12th HR of the year. It was the longest any of them had seen Bobby hit. As Bobby crossed home plate, Billy and Miquel both gave him a chest bump and the Cardinals were on their way to a "world series" victory. The final score was 8-3, but after that first inning, the Razorbacks didn't have a chance.

After the last out, the players jumped up and down, cheering and asked Coach Van where the champagne was. Most didn't even know what champagne was, but they'd seen the Royals squirt each other after they won the World Series. Coach Van gathered the team in the outfield and congratulated each boy on the team. One by one, he told a story about how each player had contributed to winning a game along the way.

When the coach got to Billy, he said, "Boys, we all know how well Billy has played all year. He's really been the leader on the team. Do you want to know why? He's worked at improving each game. No one on the team has worked as hard as Billy. He has set an example for each of you. Next year, whatever team you are playing for, work as hard as Billy has and you will be successful."

The coach ended the meeting telling everyone to get the bats and balls put away, so the coach could pack them up in his car and have them ready for next year.

"Congratulations, Team" was a big sign on the Coach Van's car as the boys took the balls and bats to it.

"How did he know?" asked Johnny.

"I guess he believed," replied Billy with a big smile on his face.""I guess he believed", replied Billy with a big smile on his face."

8

Life Changes

Miguel had moved to a house two blocks from Billy. He would ride his bike to Miguel's most days. They would play catch and eventually end up at Susie's to play a game of pickup.

Billy kept trying to get Pepsi to come out to play, but it was always, "No, I'm playing computer games."

One day, while playing pickup ball at Susie's, Bobby showed up with his face all red. He'd been crying. Everyone wanted to know what was wrong.

"Dad has been transferred to Austin, Texas, and we are moving in two weeks," cried Bobby.

Billy was stunned. Even though he'd been playing more with Miguel, Bobby was still his best friend, and before he knew it, he was crying too.

"Bobby, why does he have to be transferred?" asked Billy as tears streamed down his cheeks.

"I don't know," Bobby sobbed.

There had been bad days in Billy's life, but this was even worse than when he struck out in the championship game. His best friend was moving.

"Life is not fair," yelled Billy.

School started two weeks later. It seemed strange not to have Bobby walk or ride to school with him each day. Miguel rode with him, but it just wasn't the same as Bobby. Billy had started calling Miquel "Angel" after his middle name when he got a lucky hit one day, and the name stuck.

"Billy," said Angel on their first day of school, "I am scared to go to new school when I don't talk so well."

They had ridden for another minute before Billy answered. "I heard a saying once, Angel, that went something like this, 'the only fear we have to fear is fear itself.' I'm not really sure what it means, but I do know you got nothing to worry about."

Angel raised his eyebrows and responded like Billy had said something inspirational. "Thank you. That's good. My English will get better."

Billy liked Angel's attitude, even if his friend did feel a little self-conscious starting a new school in a new country. He wondered how he'd do if his family moved to Mexico.

Before Billy knew it, Thanksgiving had arrived. Until about two weeks earlier, his Dad had continued to work out with Billy most mornings.

On Thanksgiving afternoon, his Dad said, "Have you mastered your computer game yet?"

Billy had received the latest, coolest video game player for Christmas last year. He played for hours so he could beat Pepsi.

"You want to play me, Dad?" Billy asked, thinking his Dad would be terrible at it.

"Sure, let's do it now," his Dad responded.

Billy was shocked. His Dad beat him the first game!

"Nooo, Dad," screamed Billy, half laughing and half crying. "How did you do that?"

His Dad laughed. "I played the first sports video game called Intellivision for thousands of hours before you were born. "The graphics were not nearly as good, but a lot of the hand action was the same," explained his Dad.

The rest of the afternoon, he and his Dad played "baseball, " and with just about each pitch, his Dad would teach him something new about baseball, or the rules, or what was required to be the best. He finally beat his Dad in the third game and thereafter. He was ready for Pepsi.

Johnny joined Billy and Angel riding to school each morning, once the snow had melted and the holidays were behind them. They talked baseball; what else? Spring Training was almost here. But, once in class, Billy listened intently. He had gotten straight A's, ever since failing that first test.

One morning on the bike ride, just before practice started, Johnny said, "I think all the guys from last year's team are back with us this year so we should win the championship again."

Billy smiled and said, "Not should, we will win the championship again."

A week later, practice started, and they all saw how Billy had improved by running and using his exercise equipment every day during the winter. By the time their first game was to start, Billy felt he was ready to have a great season.

The Cardinals won their first game, 10-1. Billy led off again and was beginning to like leading off because he could steal more bases, even if he still could not wear metal spikes. As the season progressed, the team remained undefeated, and Billy was hitting over .500.

He texted Bobby, who was playing with a team in Austin, telling him about each game. Bobby would tell Billy about his games. The two of them started their contest again to determine who was the best hitter, even if it was in different leagues and different cities.

Every time Billy came to bat this year, he thought, "I need to get a hit to stay ahead of Bobby." But, even with the contest, Billy's main thrill each game came when he stole a base, which happened almost every game.

The season ended with the Cardinals winning the pennant in their division, and once again, they reached the championship game. Billy saw Mr. Treehouse sitting in the grandstands. He wondered if Mr. Treehouse had come to see him play. After the game, which the Cardinals won, 6-4, Mr. Treehouse approached Billy.

"Hi, Mr. Treehouse", Billy said.

"Hey, Billy, you remembered my name," commented Mr. Treehouse, as he put his arm around Billy's shoulder. He looked much older to Billy.

"I just wanted to let you know that I have been following you and am proud of your growth," said the Royals scout. "You've definitely learned how to hit a curve," continued the man, who had talked to Billy two years ago.

Billy really didn't know what to say but without thinking said, "I intend to play for the Royals, Mr. Treehouse, so I'm practicing every day, even in the winter." The man smiled at Billy and nodded his head. He saw a burning desire in Billy, and he liked that.

That was the last time Billy saw Mr. Treehouse and one day during the winter; his Dad told him that his friend had a heart attack and passed away. Billy was devastated. Not for Mr. Treehouse's family but because he was the only scout who had seen Billy play or so he thought.

He told his Dad that he was really sorry he'd lost his friend and then added, "Do you think other scouts will see me play?"

His Dad assured him other scouts would see him play if he kept improving like he had the past three seasons.

This winter went slowly for Billy. But his classes seemed a lot easier now as he realized the benefits of listening each day intently. It meant less time spent on homework, which meant he had more time to use the exercise equipment his Dad had gotten him. He watched videos on what major leaguers did to stay in shape to improve their game. Each time he saw a new exercise, he'd work on that for weeks at a time, and as he naturally grew in height and weight, he also grew in strength.

His favorite player, Eric Hosmer of the Royals, had several videos of what he did to improve and get stronger but he also would talk about footwork and how important that was. So Billy started doing the "dances" he saw "Hos" do, moving his feet constantly. He studied videos on running and stealing. There was no doubt in Billy's mind that he was going to be much better next year, even though he would be one of the youngest on the Spartans, the team for the 13 to 15-year-old players.

9

Mr. Booker

Billy ran almost every day after school that winter. He was determined to be the fastest baseball player ever. One day while he was running, an older man started jogging with him.

"Is your name, Billy Tankersly?" the man asked Billy.

"Yes sir, it is," replied Billy, not slowing down.

The man said he'd seen Billy running every day and knew more about him than Billy realized. "Are you a baseball player?" the man asked, already knowing the answer.

"Yes sir," Billy replied, "I'm a baseball player and intend to be the fastest player ever."

The man smiled at the young boy's confidence.

"My name is Marv Booker, and I used to be the groundskeeper for the Royals," said the graying, but athletic looking man.

"Really?" Billy questioned, stopping all of a sudden.

"I also live in Leawood, and Tom Treehouse told me about you before he had his heart attack. He would have been happy to know you are taking his advice about working hard to get better."

"I was sad about Mr. Treehouse, Mr. Booker but I am taking his advice", said Billy. Billy was in front of his house now and asked Mr. Booker if he had any ideas on how to get faster.

Mr. Booker said, with a smile on his face, "I will run with you daily and give you all the advice I can if you would like."

Billy let out an excited, "That would be great, Mr. Booker!"

He shook his hand saying it was dinner time but he would see him tomorrow after school.

"Absolutely, Billy. We will run together until the snow stops us."

Billy was thrilled as he entered the house and saw his Dad.

"You won't believe what just happened," he sputtered. "A man by the name of Mr. Booker started running with me today. He told me he had been the groundskeeper for the Royals years ago. He even knew Mr. Treehouse before he passed away. He is going to run with me every day, and coach me. He was around Major Leaguers, Dad!" Billy exclaimed, so excited he could hardly get the words out.

"Did the man happen to tell you his first name?"

"Yes sir, it was Marv."

His Dad started laughing.

"Marv Booker is the only groundskeeper in the Hall of Fame," explained his Dad.

"Hall of Fame?" Billy quizzed.

"Yes, Hall of Fame, the same as Babe Ruth, Lou Gehrig, and George Brett. He is the only groundskeeper ever to be inducted into the Hall. Major Leaguers praised his work on the field and for how much he had taught them about the right attitude to succeed", responded his Dad.

"I can't think of anyone who could teach you more about baseball and winning in all things, than Marv Booker," explained Mr. Tankersly to his son.

The next day school went by slower than ever. All Billy could think about was running with Mr. Booker and learning more about baseball.

When the school bell rang, Billy was already out the door. Mr. Booker was waiting for him.

"Did you have a good day at school, Billy?" asked the Hall of Famer. Billy nodded yes but couldn't wait to ask Mr. Booker if he was the same Marv Booker in the Hall of Fame.

"Dad told me you were in the Hall of Fame, is that right?" asked Billy.

"Yes, I got lucky on the votes, and somehow, I made it." From that moment on, Billy listened intently to every word that came out of the man's mouth as they ran together.

Every day until the first big snow storm, Billy and Mr. Booker ran after school. He learned how all the talent in the world, without the right attitude, would not attract major league scouts. He learned that the more he practiced, the better he would become. He learned to work on his strengths.

After two weeks of running at least a mile each day, Mr. Booker said, "Billy, I want to try something. I want to go to the high school baseball field and time you to first base."

For the next two weeks, Mr. Booker timed Billy running to first from the batter's box. Billy would run to first as fast as he could. Mr. Booker gave him directions, like not worrying where the ball was hit. He told Billy that he had been to one of his games with Mr. Treehouse last year. They both noticed that instead of running straight to the base, he had a habit of looking where the ball was hit, slowing him down.

Billy's time was .01 of a second faster after the second week. Mr. Booker was proud of him. Then the snowstorm hit. With 12 inches of snow on the ground, running was impossible.

10

Metal Spikes

The snow melted, but by now, it was still too cold to go out running. Mr. Tankersly watched KU games two or three times a week and once again, the Jayhawks were playing well. At one point, they were 16-0, and Billy thought, "I wish we played that many games." He was really beginning to enjoy the Jayhawks and how they worked so well as a team. Even watching basketball, Billy was thinking about baseball and teamwork.

He also watched the basketball players run up and down the court, realizing they had to run much more than baseball players. One day, he asked his Dad if they could go to a game together. His Dad explained tickets were really hard to get at the Allen Fieldhouse, where the Jayhawks played, but he would try. Sure enough, his Dad brought tickets home one night, and Billy was thrilled.

A week later, Billy got to experience the Allen Fieldhouse, which was known as one of the best atmospheres in college basketball. Seldom did the Jayhawks lose at home because the crowd was so loud and enthusiastic. Billy had never seen or heard anything like it and made up his mind if he did not get signed by a major league team, he was going to go to KU. It was the first time all winter that his mind was off baseball, even for a little while.

The Jayhawks won the National Championship that year, and Billy could not remember his Dad being that excited. His Dad was jumping up and down like a little kid. The excitement didn't wear off even the next day. All his Dad could talk about was his "National Championship Jayhawks." At the same time, all Billy could think about was "how soon will it be warm enough to run with Mr. Booker again."

Finally, it got warmer, and the snow melted. One day, Mr. Booker showed up after school.

"You ready to start running, Billy?" he asked.

Billy's face lit up like a Christmas tree.

"Yes, sir. But, I don't have my running shoes with me", said Billy.

"I have something for you. See if you can wear these."

He handed Billy a brand new pair of metal spikes. They were real metal spikes.

"Holy Smokes!" Billy whispered as he looked over the spikes.

"These are my size, but I cannot accept them," said Billy sadly.

"I know you have to wear plastic or rubber spikes right now. But, did you know there is a league where you can wear metal spikes?"

"What do you mean?" asked Billy, with an excitement level that the first men on the moon must have felt.

Mr. Booker explained that "Traveling Baseball Teams" were now the way for young players to advance more quickly.

"You need to enroll in a baseball school, Billy. You practice two days a week and play in tournaments on the weekends, plus receive private instructions on how to get better. You play about 60 games a year, travel all over and guess what? You get to wear metal spikes!"

Billy started shouting his excitement, Metal spikes, Mr. Booker?" He was not sure he'd even heard Mr. Booker right. Even college players had to wear rubber or plastic spikes.

Mr. Booker explained that baseball schools cost more. He went on to explain he had some news for Billy that would be totally unexpected. Billy didn't know what to think. "Good or bad news?" Billy thought.

Mr. Treehouse told me that had not been feeling well and he had met with his attorney, where he updated his will", continued Mr. Booker. "He ended up passing away about two weeks after he signed his new will, so it was like he knew something bad was going on. But he told me he changed his will, which even surprised me", added Mr. Booker, with a twinkle in his eye.

"Billy, Mr. Treehouse was very impressed with you as a fine young man. He felt you had good character and were talented enough to be a professional baseball player one day if you devoted yourself to it. He told me he wanted to help you get better. That is when he explained he had not been feeling well and wanted me to know what he was planning."

"Do you know what a will is?" he asked.

"I've heard that word, Mr. Booker, but don't really understand", Billy answered.

Mr. Booker explained to Billy that when someone passes away, they have a piece of paper called a will that directs the attorney how to divide up the money or property. Most the time, the inheritance would go to the person's spouse or children but in this case, Mr. Treehouse's wife passed away before him, and they had no children. The majority of his money was going to a trust fund to help young boys in the Kansas City area become better players.

"He set it up for you to be the first recipient and it will include all expenses for you to play in the traveling baseball league, with a membership to the Baseball Academy of Leawood."

"Really?" asked Billy.

"This will cover all of your baseball expenses until you are 17 years old. I've talked to Mr. Elton, the owner of the baseball school and one of their teams still needs a shortstop. Most of the teams are already filled with players but this team's shortstop ended up having to move and the coach, Mr. Jake Heier has not found a suitable replacement. He has agreed to have you try out for the team next week if you want to do so", continued Mr. Booker.

Billy stood still. He didn't know what to think. All that came to his mind was, "Metal Spikes."

11

Invited

Billy's excitement immediately turned to fear.

"Leave Angel and his other friends?" thought Billy. He didn't know if he could or not, but metal spikes?

Mr. Booker walked Billy home. He told Billy more about the team and traveling baseball. He learned he would be playing with better players, all who aspired to play college or pro ball.

As they walked toward the front door, Billy's Dad came out and greeted Mr. Booker with a firm handshake. He offered Mr. Booker to stay and to have dinner. Billy's mom, Julie, had already set a place for Mr. Booker at the table, which Billy thought was strange. He learned over dinner that Mr. Booker had met with his Dad that afternoon before he ran with Billy.

"Billy," his Dad began. "I knew Mr. Treehouse really liked you but had no idea about the Trust Fund in his will until today. He told me last year that you were someone he could really get behind because of your character."

Mr. Tankersly continued, "Tom said last summer he was going to help you reach your full potential. When I heard the news that he'd passed away, I was disappointed for you because I felt he was someone who could really help you achieve your goal. The news from Mr. Booker today shocked me. First, I never dreamed Tom would pass away so suddenly, and second, he never told me about his plans for a Trust

Fund. But, I don't know if this is the best thing for you", questioned his Dad.

"Do you want to be on a traveling baseball team that would mean leaving your old friends?" asked his mom.

Billy thought before answering, "Mom, after talking to Mr. Booker today, if it meant better coaching for me, major league scouts coming to the tournaments and being able to wear metal spikes, I would do it."

His mind had not left the fact that he could finally wear metal spikes. He did not like the fact that he would be playing on a team without his friends, but after Bobby had moved away, he learned that he was good at making new friends.

Dinner ended with Mr. Booker telling the family that the Yankees, one of the teams from the Baseball Academy was looking for a shortstop. The coach would hold a tryout, measuring the five tools that all pro baseball teams look for, running, hitting, hitting for power, fielding, and throwing.

That meant that even if Billy tried out, he might not make the team, but if he did well, it sounded like he would be starting. Mr. Booker hugged Billy goodbye and headed home, which Billy learned was only about two blocks away. Billy held up his new pair of spikes, waving to the man who changed his life, in one day.

"Dad and Mom," asked Billy once he got back inside. "What do you think?"

Julie spoke first, "Billy, I know how much you like Angel and the rest of the guys, but I worry about this hurting your friendships. You are the young man who wouldn't even move up to the Cardinals a couple of years ago because you didn't want to hurt the team."

His Dad chimed in, "Your Mom is right, playing in the traveling baseball league would mean that you won't get to see your old friends very much."

Billy remained quiet and thought, "Metal spikes, major league scouts, and 60 games being played."

He was pretty sure his mind was already made up, but he wanted to talk to his best friend before making his final decision.

"Dad, Mom, I'm going to my room to Skype Bobby," he told them.

"Hey, what's up?" Billy asked as they were connected.

He and Bobby had maintained their friendship through texting, Facebook, and Skyping about once a week since Bobby had moved to Austin.

"Something really exciting happened last week," exclaimed Bobby. "I got invited to try out for a traveling baseball team, and I made the team," he almost shouted.

"What?" Billy said, with his voice sounding more like a teenage girl's scream.

"Have you heard of traveling baseball teams, Billy?"

"Yes, I have," answered Billy without telling him he'd been invited to do the same.

For the next five minutes, Billy couldn't get a word in edgewise. Bobby just kept telling him about traveling baseball, the fact they got to wear metal spikes, use wooden bats and play all over the country. He told Billy that for the first time ever, he was glad his Dad had taken that higher paying job in Austin because otherwise, he wouldn't be able to do this because of the cost.

"Well, Bobby, I've got some news too," he finally butted in. "I've been invited to try out for a traveling team also. I don't really know much about it, but some man left me like a scholarship for the Baseball Academy of Leawood. I really don't know if I should accept it or not."

"Heck, yes you should!" Bobby shouted.

"I probably will," Billy replied, still thinking about having to leave his friends.

After another 20 minutes talking to Bobby, Billy's mind was made up. He was going to try out for the Yankees and hopefully, get to wear the metal spikes Mr. Booker had given him. Billy went running to the living room.

"My mind's made up, I'm going to do it," he told his Dad and Mom.

The next day, he ran with Mr. Booker, telling him that he definitely wanted to try out for the Yankees and quizzed the man about what he needed to do. Mr. Booker explained that it was already set up.

"Next week, after school on Monday, you are to go to the Baseball Academy of Leawood. The owner, Mr. Elton, will introduce you to Coach Jake Heier, who is the manager of the Yankees. He will measure you in the essential tools I explained yesterday. Once you make the team, they will measure you twice a year in each category, as well as measure your height and weight. They will keep and share these records with major league scouts", explained Mr. Booker.

All Billy could think about the rest of the week was trying out for the Yankees. Yet, as excited as he was, there was no way he could tell his friends about the

Yankees. He was picturing starting at shortstop and stealing more bases in his metal spikes than anyone else ever had in traveling baseball.

12

Try Out

At school, Monday was the longest day he'd ever spent. It was like he wasn't hearing his teachers at all, even though he'd prided himself on being a good listener. His mind was on one thing; traveling baseball. After school, Mr. Booker picked him up, and they drove to the Baseball Academy.

"Billy, there is no need for you to be nervous," Mr. Booker encouraged. "You will pass the tests with flying colors, and Coach Heier is going to be thrilled the day you joined the team."

Billy carried his spikes over his shoulder as they entered the huge building with big red letters on top saying, "Baseball Academy of Leawood, The Home of Future Stars." Billy was impressed the minute they walked in the door. There had to be at least four batting cages, but no sooner than he saw all the activity inside, Mr. Elton came out to meet Billy. He obviously already knew Marv Booker. "After all, he was in the Hall of Fame," Billy thought.

Mr. Booker introduced the two of them. Billy wondered how much Mr. Booker had already told the owner, but his thought was broken as a cheerful younger man came up and asked, "Is this the Billy Tankersly I've heard about?"

Mr. Booker introduced Billy to Coach Heier as Billy thought, "This coach isn't nearly as old as my other coaches."

He quickly learned that Coach Heier had played baseball at the University of Texas, which was in

Austin, the same city Bobby lived in. He had been a pitcher and was on his way to the majors. After two years in the minors, he learned he was going to have "Tommy John" surgery on his elbow, and that ended his career. Billy had heard of "Tommy John" surgery but thought that most pitchers came back to be able to pitch again. He learned that Coach Heier tried a comeback but just did not have the arm speed ever to make the majors, so he decided to coach a travel baseball team and to work with young kids.

"OK, Billy, let's get started," the young coach instructed. "First, I want to time you running to 1st base and measure your speed." Billy was glad that was the first test because after all the running he had done with Mr. Booker, he knew he would do well. The coach told Billy to go ahead and warm up, and when he was ready, they would begin the tests.

Coach Heier was amazed when he timed Billy running to first. His speed was 4.2 seconds, which rated far above average for players Billy's age.

"Now I want you to hit and then run," Coach said. "Holy Smokes, Billy!" the coach yelled. "Even hitting the ball first, you ran it in 4.1 seconds. That's great! A 3.9 for a left-handed hitter is considered an "8" on a major league's scouting report. An "8" is the best score you can get. By the time you are 16 with proper training, you should be breaking 3.9", he added. "Let's time you from first to third base now," the coach said.

His time to third base had Coach Heier laughing, telling Mr. Booker, "You weren't kidding about Billy being fast."

The 13-year-old was proud and also very thankful that Mr. Booker had worked with him because he was not that fast before they started working on his base running.

"Have you ever tried drag bunting?" the coach asked.

"No sir," Billy replied.

"OK, let me show you."

He got in the batter's box, and as soon as the pitch was thrown, the coach started running as his bat softly hit the ball down the first-base line.

"That's how you do it. Now would you try it for me?"

Billy tried and missed the first pitch completely. He felt embarrassed, but the coach said, "Try it again, Billy."

Almost as soon as the pitcher released the ball, Billy was running trying to bunt the ball at the same time. He did it and reached first base in 3.8 seconds. The coach was amazed and let it be known.

"That was the fastest time I've ever seen from a 13-year-old", grinned the coach. "In fact, the fastest any major leaguer has ever been timed was Joel Thompson, who was clocked at 3.3 seconds although no one really believed it."

Billy was beaming. He knew his metal spikes made all the difference.

"Now, let's focus on your hitting," the coach said. He continued, "I want to see you take ten swings but do not swing unless the ball is over the plate."

Billy thought, "He didn't need to say that."

He hit seven of the pitches for what he considered to be base hits but he knew the coach was evaluating his power so he tried to hit with as much power as he could, without swinging and missing. Two of his hits went over the short fence in right field, which was the practice diamond inside the building. Billy was sure they would have been long fly balls in traveling baseball, but he still felt good after taking his swings.

All the coach said was, "Good."

"Let's see how you field, Billy," said Coach Heier.

Billy got his glove and ran out to the shortstop position. After about ten grounders to his right and left, the coach hit a ball hard, directly at him. Billy stayed in front of it, but the ball took a bad bounce and bounced off his chest. He then picked it up as fast as he could and threw a strike to first base.

"Nice one!" the coach shouted. "Good arm too."

After the tryout was over, Coach Heier approached Billy who was taking off his spikes.

"Billy, the Yankees would be proud to have you on our team," he said.

Mr. Booker drove Billy home. He was almost as excited as Billy.

"You did great," he told the youngster.

When they pulled into Billy's driveway, Jim was waiting outside for them.

"How'd you do?" he asked, as excited to hear the results as Billy was to tell him.

Billy said with a big smile on his face, "I'm a Yankee, Dad!"

13

Big Decision

After telling his Mom and then Skyping Bobby to tell him the news, he realized he had to tell Angel and all his friends, as well as the coach of the Spartans. He dreaded telling Angel most of all. Billy went to sleep that night, excited and scared. He did not want to tell Angel.

As they rode their bikes to school the next morning, Billy broke the news.

"Angel, I've got something to tell you. I'm not going to be playing on the Spartans this year", Billy almost whispered.

"What?" Angel yelled. "Why not?" asked Angel, sort of mad, sad and confused.

Billy explained as much as he could. He wasn't going to tell him about Mr. Treehouse, so he just told Angel he'd been invited to the Leawood Baseball Academy and that his Dad paid for it, saying "this is your Birthday and Christmas present."

He felt bad saying that because it was a lie. Angel was completely silent on the rest of the way to school.

When they got there, Billy said, "Angel, I told you a little lie. Dad isn't paying for the Academy. Remember that Scout I told you about? Well, he passed away and left me a scholarship. It was a complete shock to me, but he had talked to Dad and Mr. Booker before he died. He told them both that he wanted to help me get better. Apparently, this was his way of helping kids, and I happened to be the first recipient. I tried out for a traveling baseball team yesterday, where they get to wear real metal spikes and hit with wooden bats. I made the team, and it was the last position available this year."

Angel smiled, didn't say a word and walked down the hall to his class in the opposite direction. He was obviously hurt. His best friend wouldn't be playing with him this year or maybe ever again. Billy saw Angel during lunch, but Angel still didn't say a word to him. Angel didn't even look at Billy, which made him feel even worse. He was beginning to wonder if he had made the right decision or not. School was out, and Billy was happy to see Mr. Booker waiting for him.

"Mr. Booker, I really hurt Angel's feelings today when I told him about the Yankees", Billy told his running coach. "I am having second thoughts."

"Billy put your spikes on and let's run," Mr. Booker instructed.

As they ran, Mr. Booker acted like Billy's dad. "Your father told me something about you, Billy that you probably don't know. I know how bad you felt when your best friend Bobby moved to Austin. Now, I have a question for you. Did you and Bobby stop being friends once he'd moved?" Mr. Booker asked.

"No sir," Billy replied, knowing that Mr. Booker was going to tell him that he and Angel would still be friends. He knew what he would say to Angel tomorrow, and now it was time to learn to run faster.

"OK, Mr. Booker, how do I improve my speed?" he asked.

"Billy, I've told you all winter. You do everything you can to strengthen your legs, not just by running but by using the exercise equipment your Dad got you", Mr. Booker answered.

Billy was determined to be the fastest baseball player ever and was willing to do whatever was necessary. That night, after he'd run with Mr. Booker, Billy spent the rest the night on the exercise equipment trying to build up his leg strength.

Coach Heier made sure that Billy knew the practice was Friday night at 5:00 PM sharp. The rest of the week could not pass fast enough. He did talk to Angel the next morning and explained they'd still be best friends, and Angel seemed to be OK with that, but he was still sad. Finally, Friday came, and Mr. Booker took Billy to practice.

The first thing Coach Heier did was introduce Billy to the other kids on the Yankee's team. They didn't look any different than other boys his age although he learned that some were 14 years old. He was as big as them he thought. Billy had a hard time remembering each kid's name, but when they took infield practice, he realized that Tommy Johnston played second base and Will Harsh played first base. Bill Hagara played third base, so there were two "Billys" on the infield.

"How he would know if the Coach was yelling at him or the other Bill?"

The coach was ahead of him.

"Billy Tankersly, you are going to be Billy and Bill Hagara, I'm going to call you Butch," said the coach.

"Butch?" Bill Hagara asked, with a frown on his face.

"For two reasons, Butch," the coach answered with a smile on his face. "First off, Butch Thompson was my best friend and the star athlete at our high school. Second, you remind me of him at your age. So, do you mind if I call you Butch?" the coach asked.

Bill Hagara smiled and wondered if he'd be known as Butch the rest of his life?

"Nope, Coach, I don't mind a bit. From now on, I'm Butch", he said with a big smile.

Coach Heier went around the infield hitting grounders to each boy. Butch made a nice pickup on the first ball hit to him and rifled it across to first. Billy was amazed at Butch's arm. Then came a grounder to him and he handled it flawlessly. Tommy had to hustle to his left to get the grounder Coach Heier hit to him and Will Harsh at first made a backhanded play on a grounder to his left. Will was left-handed, so the ball was just barely fair.

Billy thought, "The coach did that on purpose, to check Will's footwork at first base."

When they got to turning double plays, Billy realized Tommy was far better than anyone he'd played with, and he transferred the ball out of his hand almost as fast as Billy did when he was playing second. He wasn't going to admit that maybe Tommy did it faster. What happened next surprised them all. The coach had them go to deep center field and throw all the way to the plate. Butch's throw bounced once and hit the catcher perfectly. Billy couldn't remember the catcher's name, but Butch yelled out, "Jose, was the runner out?" Jose gave a "safe" sign to Butch, razzing him. This was a little different atmosphere than with his other teams. He remembered the coaches disapproved of razzing but here, it seemed to be OK.

Butch laughed at Jose and yelled, "You're blind, ump."

Then it was Billy's turn to throw it all the way to the plate. He threw it as hard as he could. It sailed over Jose's out-stretched glove by two feet. Butch, Tommy, Will and Jose all started laughing and calling him Gus, in honor of an outfielder in the majors who was known for overthrowing a base.

Billy yelled to the coach, "Let me have another try!"

The coach was talking to his pitchers and shouted "OK" without really paying attention, but he had seen Billy's first throw and heard the kids laughing. Billy was determined to make his next throw to the plate, every bit as on the mark as Butch's. He was focused. He glared at Jose and visualized his throw hitting the glove right over the heart of the plate. He watched his throw hit Jose's mitt without bouncing and could hear Jose yelling, "Safe."

Billy knew he was part of the team when Jose did that, so he yelled back at Jose, "You need to get your eyes examined."

He was beginning to like the razzing.

The coach had them run to first. Billy didn't know what his time was, but he knew he was the fastest. Tommy and Butch were fast, but it took all he had to keep from laughing as Jose ran to first. He was very, very slow. Then the coach had them run three laps around the bases and two laps around the outfield. Billy finished first each lap and after the outfield laps was 20 feet ahead of Tommy who finished second. He was exhausted. He ran as hard as he could each lap. Mr. Treehouse and Mr. Booker would have been proud of him.

Practice came to an end with Coach Heier telling them that their first tournament was next weekend in Wichita, Kansas. Billy was excited to play his very first game with metal spikes.

14

First Tournament

The Yankees had one more practice before their first tournament. It was like the first one, and at the end, Coach Heier gave each boy a map of how to get to the baseball field in Wichita, along with the brackets. They would play three games with the last one being for the tournament championship if they won their first two. If they lost, they still got to play the doubleheader on Saturday and the single game on Sunday for a consolation prize.

Coach Heier told the team, "You boys are good. With the exception of Billy, you guys have been practicing together for a month and are good enough to win this first tournament."

The team all put their hands together and shouted "Yankees" as each boy left for home. Billy's dad and Mr. Booker were waiting outside for him as he left the building.

"How'd practice go?" his Dad asked.

"Good, Dad," Billy responded, but he was thinking of actually playing a game in his metal spikes. Mr. Tankersly looked over to Mr. Booker and asked if he was riding to Wichita with them for the tournament.

"I'd love to, Jim," he replied.

"We are going down Friday night and will be staying at the Holiday Inn Friday and Saturday. Do you want me to book you a room?" Billy's Dad asked.

"That would be great. Just let me know how much it costs", replied Mr. Booker as he got out of the car at his home.

Friday finally arrived. Billy, his Dad and Mom, and Mr. Booker were on their way to Wichita, Kansas. Billy read someplace that the Flint Hills of Kansas had the best sunset in the world. Looking out of the window of the back seat, he saw a sign, "Flint Hills" and it was right at sunset. He looked around him, and the entire sky was a bright orange.

He thought, "Whoever viewed sunsets all around the world had to really search because the Flint Hills are out in the middle of nowhere."

But, this sunset was like none he'd ever seen. For a good 30 minutes, everyone in the car was spellbound by the beauty, but all Billy could think about was, "How much further to Wichita?"

As they checked into the hotel, Billy saw Butch and his family.

"Hey, Billy!" Butch yelled across the lobby. "Are you going swimming?" he asked.

Billy knew there was an indoor pool, but he had been so focused on the game that he forgot his swimming trunks.

"Nope, Butch," Billy yelled. "Going to spit-shine my spikes."

At 9:00 AM, the team starting arriving at McClutchen Field. Billy was the first one there, and he studied the field. He'd only played on an infield with grass a couple of times so he ran out to his position and imagined balls being hit to him, wondering what effect the grass would have on the grounders hit his way.

"Hey Billy," he heard his coach yell. "Come over here for a minute."

Billy ran to the group surrounding the coach.

"Listen, guys; I just found out who the Gator's pitcher will be for the first game. His name is Tad Jones, and he throws a wicked changeup. I remember seeing him last year, and the secret to hitting him is to hit his fastball", concluded the coach.

Butch, Billy, Tommy, and Will took the field for infield practice, and the grass infield did make the ball bounce differently, but none of the guys had any major problems.

"Tommy, who's that girl that came with you?" Billy asked.

"My sister," Tommy replied.

"She just gave me a shiny coin and told me to put it in my pocket because it would bring me good luck," said Billy.

Tommy said, "She has given every player a new coin telling them the same thing."

Billy laughed saying, "Guess we should win this tournament then." Then the coach called them to go over the lineup.

Billy was batting leadoff with Garrett Richardson, the centerfielder, batting second followed by Butch and Will. Tommy was hitting sixth right behind the right fielder, Santiago Torrez. Jose was batting seventh, and Mateo Cruz, the left fielder batting eighth. Pitching the first game was Jon Heath, who was 14 and had a fastball better than any Billy had seen.

The Yankees were listed as the visitors in this first game, so Billy was the first to bat.

"Come on, Billy," Butch yelled. "Get it started."

Billy did just that. He saw his pitch, a fastball about belt high. He lashed a single to right field, stole second, and came in to score on Garrett's double. He knew his metal spikes had allowed him to beat the throw to the plate. Butch doubled, making the score 2-0 with no outs.

"What's the matter Pitch, can't you get anyone out," yelled Santiago. It was obvious; the pitcher had rabbit ears because he looked over at the Yankee bench as Santiago was yelling. Once he did that, it seemed like the entire team started razzing him. The Yankees batted around that first inning and led 7-0 before the Gators even got up to the plate. The final score was 10-1, and the team had an hour to rest before their second game of the day. Billy had never played in a double header.

"Hey Garrett, have you ever played a doubleheader before?" asked Billy.

"Yep, we had quite a few last year, in fact, almost every weekend," Garrett replied. Billy felt a little foolish because he knew Garrett was on last year's Yankee team and all the tournaments had double headers.

"Duh," he thought. "That was a stupid question."

In the second game, rain started coming down just after Billy had once again opened the game with a single. It wasn't a heavy rain, but the base paths were getting a little muddy. Billy looked over for the steal sign, but the coach didn't give it. The next three Yankees struck out, and Billy was stranded at first base.

By the time Billy came up to bat again, the Bullets had led the game 2-0, and the rain had stopped. Coach Heier came over to him before the inning started.

"Billy, we need runners on base, and I want you to drag bunt down the first base line," instructed the coach.

The first pitch was a fastball, high and inside. The second pitch was a changeup that Billy laid off of, and the umpire yelled, "Strike one." On the next pitch, Billy expected a fastball and placed it perfectly down the first baseline while already starting to run. The Bullets didn't even try to throw to first as Billy crossed the bag in less than 4.0 seconds. He got the steal sign on Garrett's first pitch and was running once the pitcher's leg crossed the rubber. "Safe!" yelled the ump. That was the start of a four-run rally, and the Yankees won the game 8-3. Billy had three hits and three stolen bases.

"Guys," Coach Heier started their post-game meeting. "We played good baseball today and tomorrow will be playing the Shockers, who also won two games today. Get some sleep tonight so we can win this tournament", the coach concluded. He didn't mention any individual but played up the teamwork he'd seen that entire day. Billy and Tommy turned two double plays, one in each game, and had not made an error. Billy rode back to the hotel with his Dad, Mom, and Mr. Booker, who he'd heard cheering all day long. He was happy about making the decision to play for the Yankees, even though he missed Angel and his last year's teammates.

The championship game Sunday was a run-away and not in the Yankees favor. The Shockers were more like a professional team. Every one of their players got a hit that Sunday afternoon and Jack Hughes, who was the starting pitcher for the Yankees just could not stop the Shockers. Billy got one hit, stole two bases but didn't score. In fact, the Yankees didn't score at all. The final was 10-0, in favor of the Shockers. After the game, Coach Heier was obviously disappointed.

"OK, guys, did you feel better after the games yesterday or today?" the Coach asked.

"Yesterday," the team chimed in unison. "So we agree that winning is better than losing, right?" asked the coach.

"Yes," shouted everyone on the team.

Then Coach Heier started telling each of the players how they could improve. When he got to Billy, he said, "You did not make any errors but you let two ground balls get by you on your left that you could have reached if you'd been hustling."

Billy had never in his life been accused of not hustling, and Coach Heier saw the "question-mark" look in Billy's eyes.

"Let me explain, Billy," he said. "Maybe hustling isn't the word I'm looking for. You were hustling but because of the grass infield, I suppose, you were playing closer in than back at home in our practices, and the balls got by you."

Billy spoke up. "Coach, I really was hustling, but you are right. I think I edged in a bit because of the grass, thinking that it would slow the ball down but I don't think it did because those two hits you are talking about just got by me, almost before I could react", defended Billy.

"After the first one got by you, you should have realized that due to the rain, the ball was scooting on the grass faster than normal. Baseball is a thinking man's game, and you have to be on your toes all the time. I know you have the talent, but you have got to play smart", concluded the coach.

Billy made up his mind, never again would he be accused of not playing smart baseball.

On the drive home, his dad turned on a Royals broadcast, and they all listened to the game, all except for Billy. He was replaying every pitch in that last game, trying to figure out how to get better.

15

Mow Yards

The next weekend, they played much closer to home at Paola, Kansas. Paola had long had a team that won almost every tournament. It was a farming community and "these farm boys know how to play baseball," thought Billy after the tournament concluded. The Yankees won their first two games like last weekend but lost the Sunday game to the Paola Panthers.

Billy had a total of five hits in the three games and stole six bases. He was convinced that no one could throw him out in his metal spikes, but the feeling of losing made him forget about what he'd done. He went to sleep that night, visualizing pitches that he'd taken, thinking, "I should have swung at that one. It was a home run pitch", was his last thought before falling asleep.

Monday afternoon after Billy's Dad got home from work; he called Billy out to the garage.

"Billy, you are 13 years old. You are a great kid, but you need to have something other than baseball in your life. I'm going to buy a lawn mower for you, and I want you to start mowing yards."

Billy stood in silence, not knowing what to say.

His Dad continued, "Son, I want you to go to each house on our block and the one behind us. I want you to sell your lawn mowing services, set up a schedule for everyone you sign up, and mow at least four yards a day."

Billy screamed at the top of his lungs, "Dad, I can't do that and still focus on baseball."

Jim Tankersly replied, "Billy, not only can you do it, you are going to do it. After you mow the yards, you are going to collect your money, set up a bank account, do your own books and pay me back for the lawnmower."

Billy looked stunned. He didn't even know what "doing his own books" meant, and there was no way he could mow four yards a day and still be sharp at baseball practice or in the games.

His Dad was unrelenting. Billy cried and threw a temper tantrum.

"Why, Dad," Bill screamed. "How is that going to help me be a major leaguer?" he shouted.

"Billy," his Dad answered, "it is going to teach you how to sell, how to start a business of your own, how to keep books and most of all, it's going to make you 'think' all the time. You are going to have to think about what yards you have to mow each day, how are you going to get done fast enough to make practice, and probably the most important of all, it is going to teach you the value of money."

Billy went to sleep that night, hoping his Dad would forget this crazy notion about him mowing yards.

Practice the next day found Billy still thinking about what his Dad was demanding. He missed several ground balls in infield practice and didn't hit a ball out of the infield during batting practice. Coach Heier called him over after practice to ask him what was wrong.

"Billy, something is bothering you, what is it?" asked the coach.

Billy's emotions exploded about what his Dad wanted him to do. Coach Heier didn't help. He told Billy that every young man had to learn responsibility because not all kids would reach the major leagues. They had to be prepared for another career.

Billy just looked at him before, in a loud voice, saying, "Mowing yards?" Coach Heier had a hard time to keep from laughing but explained to Billy that there was another thing he had to learn. Billy looked at him and said, "What?"

"You have to learn to deal with authority." Billy looked puzzled, "what does that mean, Coach?" "It means obeying your Father and Mother, your coaches, and someday, your boss, whether it's the manager of a major league team or a boss at a job you might someday have if you don't make the majors."

Billy rolled his eyes and told the coach, "I am going to make the majors, Coach."

Coach Heier said in a firm tone, "Maybe," but this year, it sounds like you are going to be mowing yards."

The next morning, his Dad woke him early and said, "OK Billy, you need to get up and start going to each neighbor on this block to ask if you can mow their yards."

Billy was still half asleep as he got dressed and knocked on the next door neighbor's front door.

"Hi Billy, how are you doing?" asked Mrs. Hansen.

"I'm doing OK. Dad wants me to get a lawn mowing route before I can practice baseball each day. Do you need your yard mowed every week this summer?" asked Billy.

"How much do you charge?" Mrs. Hansen asked.

"Heck, I don't know, Mr. Hansen. What about $2.00?"

"Billy, that is not enough. You need to charge more. I'll tell you what I'll do. I will pay you $5.00 a week to mow my yard, but if it's not perfect, I'm going to call you to have you re-do it", Mrs. Hansen told him.

Billy told her he would start tomorrow as his Dad was buying the lawn mower today. She seemed happy with that, so Billy went to the next house on the block. This was Mr. Green's house, and Billy for some reason had always been a little afraid of Mr. Green. One day, Billy threw a ball to Pepsi, and Pepsi missed it. It went into Mr. Green flower garden. When Billy went to get the ball, Mr. Green came out and told him to get out of his flower bed. Ever since then, he'd been a little afraid of Mr. Green.

"Mr. Green, I'm starting a lawn mowing business, and would like to mow your yard weekly", Billy started. Before Mr. Green could ask, Billy said, "I charge $10 a week."

The youngster was learning about money. Mr. Green agreed, and after covering the entire block, on both sides of the street, he had four people who had decided to pay him to mow their yards. All except Mrs. Hansen were going to pay Billy $10 a week. When he got home, he Skyped Bobby, telling him what all had happened the past two weeks, mostly complaining about having to mow yards.

"Billy, I have to mow yards too," Bobby told him. "I've already made $250, and am putting it in a savings account at the bank."

Billy looked at Bobby on the Skype screen, feeling a little better if his best friend had to do the same thing.

"So how many yards do you mow?" Billy asked. "I mow five yards a day, four days a week," responded Bobby.

"I just don't want to do that," whined Billy.

"Hey buddy, I never hear you complain. Don't you remember our first coach, Coach Yam, who insisted that he never wanted to hear us complain, condemn or criticize?" Bobby reminded Billy.

After hanging up, Billy thought about what Bobby had said. The fact that Bobby was mowing more yards than his Dad asked him to do made him wonder if he could do more than four a day. He certainly didn't want Bobby to make more money than him this summer. His competitiveness had kicked in. No way was he going to lose to Bobby.

When his Dad got home with "his" new mower, he tried it out on their yard, after his Dad went through about a million safety tips. Billy found out it was not as hard as he expected. He didn't tell his Dad, but he was determined to sell more people the next day, and make more money that Bobby.

16

Opportunity In Problems

Billy started the next morning mowing the four neighbor's yards that had agreed to have him mow all summer. He charged all of them $10 plus Mrs. Hansen's $5.00, and by lunch time, he already had mowed each yard and collected $35.00. He made up his mind to sell two more before practice. On his bike, he rode to the neighbors behind their house, and within 20 minutes had two more customers.

"This could be sort of fun, but I've got to make more money than Bobby," thought Billy.

He decided to go to one more house. He didn't know their name but rang the doorbell, and a sweet woman came to the door.

He introduced himself and asked if she would be interested in having her yard mowed weekly.

She asked, "How much do you charge, Billy?"

Without thinking, he said, "I charge $15 a week."

She agreed, and Billy went home realizing that he just added another $35 once he mowed their yards, and that was $35 for three yards instead of four like he'd already done today. Billy was pretty jazzed as Mr. Booker took him to practice.

Once Billy explained to Mr. Booker about his lawn mowing route, Mr. Booker said, "Billy, I am really proud of you." Mowing yards will strengthen your legs and help you get faster."

"Wow," thought Billy. He hadn't even considered that.

At practice, he fielded every ground ball cleanly, even making a couple of plays that the coach yelled out, "Nice play, Billy." When he hit, for the first time all year, he was spraying the ball to all fields.

Coach Heier walked over to the batting cage and asked, "Where did you learn to hit like that, Billy?"

Billy told him that his slow-pitch coach had taught him to hit to left to raise his batting average.

"That was the best you've hit since coming out for the team, Billy. If you keep hitting like that, you can break every stolen base record in traveling baseball, simply because you are going to be on base so often."

The smile on Billy's face probably could have been seen from the International Space Station that Billy had seen fly across the sky one night. Mr. Booker wasn't there after practice, so Billy ran home, excited to tell his Dad that he'd mowed four yards that day and sold three more.

Mr. Booker was at his house when he got home. Billy didn't realize, but Mr. Booker had two kids of his own, from his ex-wife. Billy didn't know Mr. Booker had an ex-wife. He found out that one of his boys had been in an accident, and Mr. Booker was headed to Denver, where his son was in a hospital.

"Marv, if there is anything we can do, let us know," said Billy's Dad.

"You can take me to the airport, Jim, if you don't mind," said Mr. Booker.

Billy didn't know if he should ask to go or not. "Dad, do you want me to ride with you?" he asked finally.

"No son, you stay here and help your Mom with the laundry," Mr. Tankersly told his son.

Billy was dying to tell his Dad about his mowing experiences, but it was going to have to wait. Apparently, Mr. Booker's flight was late, and Billy had to go to bed before his Dad got home. The next morning, he got up almost excited about mowing more yards, knowing it was strengthening his legs. His Dad had already left for work, but Billy wondered if his Mom had told his Dad about the mowing that night. "No matter," he thought.

"I'll have more yards after today and Dad will be shocked," thought Billy. He mowed his three yards and then canvassed the other side of that block. He got three more sales, and all were for $15 each.

With no practice that night, Billy knew he'd be able to brag about his lawn mowing service when his Dad got home. He Skyped Bobby.

"Hey Bobby," he said when Bobby picked up. "I've sold ten people so far, mowed seven in two days and have three more to mow tomorrow." Bobby was impressed.

"That's great, Billy. Your attitude seems to be much better too, as you're not complaining, but rejoicing", smiled Bobby.

"How much did you charge?" Bobby asked.

Billy told him and found out that Bobby had been charging $10 for every yard.

"Heck Billy, at this rate, you're going to make more money this summer than me," complained Bobby.

Bobby realized that it sounded like he was complaining, so he reversed his direction and told Billy, "I'm going to get more yards. No way are you going to earn more this summer than me."

Billy laughed, and said, "Oh yes I am, Bobby. I've got the hang of this now."

Both boys laughed at how competitive they still were, miles and miles apart and for something other than baseball. After hanging up, Billy started waiting for his Dad to get home.

No sooner than his Dad walked in, Billy was telling him, "Thanks Dad for making me cut lawns. I'm actually excited about it", he added.

His Dad was sort of dumbfounded. He became more serious than normal and said, "Son, have you been doing drugs?" Billy laughed, thinking it was funny that his Dad would ask him such a stupid question, and seem to be sincere about it.

"No Dad, I am not doing drugs," he said, still laughing.

His Dad got even more suspicious, and said, "Billy, I know kids your age smoke marijuana. Have you smoked it?"

"NO Dad, I'm excited because Bobby and I have a contest to see who can earn the most money this year. He's mowing yards too, and right now, I already have ten customers for $105 each week", Billy told his Dad, still excited.

Mr. Tankersly finally relaxed enough to congratulate his son, and that made Billy proud.

He continued, "Also Dad, Mr. Booker told me that mowing lawns would strengthen my legs, which will make me faster."

By now, Billy's Dad saw that he really was excited about mowing yards, and all he could think was, "what a difference a day makes in a teenager's life."

17

Best News

The following week, the Yankees played in a tournament close to Kansas City. It was in Leavenworth, Kansas. Billy knew about Leavenworth because the State Penitentiary was located there, and his Dad had told him when he was 11 that they were thinking about bringing terrorists from Guantanamo to the United States to hold them at the Penitentiary. He didn't know if that had happened, but it was sort of scary. They drove by the Penitentiary on the way to the field.

Tommy saw Billy first.

"Billy, Billy, have you heard?" asked Tommy.

"Heard what, I just got here?" said Billy puzzled.

"We are going to play a tournament in Austin, Texas on a minor league field," said Tommy excitedly.

"Austin," Billy screamed.

"Yes, it is the field of the Round Rock Express, the Triple A club of the Texas Rangers," said Tommy, not understanding Billy's unusual way of responding.

"All you can say is, Austin?" asked Tommy.

"Yes, Tommy, that's all I can say because my best friend from my first three teams lives there now, and we Skype all the time. I am super excited, but he didn't say anything yesterday, so I guess we will not be playing his team, but that would be super exciting", answered Billy.

Tommy smiled and went over to Butch telling him the news. Billy just stood there, thinking about playing against Bobby. He hoped even if it was a small hope that they would get to play each other.

Before he knew it, the game was starting, and he hit a hard double down the right field line his first time up and then promptly stole third base. Garrett hit a high fly ball to shallow center, and Billy tagged up heading for the plate. His head was down, but he could see the catcher getting ready to catch the throw. At the last second, he dove for the plate on the outside part and reached out with his hand to tag it. The catcher put the ball on him as soon as he touched the back of the plate and he heard the umpire yell, "Safe."

From that point on, the Yankees played their best baseball of the season and won all three games. Billy had been the star of the weekend with seven hits, five stolen bases, and five runs. He even drove in two runs with another double.

On the way home, Billy told his Dad and Mom about playing in two weeks in Austin, Texas. They were both excited because they knew Billy would get to see Bobby.

His Dad said, "Billy, what if we leave a day early so you can spend time with Bobby?"

Billy was excited. The first thing he did when arriving home was Skype Bobby.

18

Austin Trip

Bobby's Skype number rang and rang, but Bobby didn't pick up. Billy hung up, disappointed he didn't get to talk to Bobby to let him know the news. Just then, his Skype number rang and it was Bobby.

"Sorry, Billy, I couldn't get to the computer fast enough," apologized Bobby.

"Bobby, I have a question for you. Look at your schedule. Does your team happen to play at the Round Rock Express Stadium in two weeks?" he asked.

"I don't know, Billy. I'll have to get my schedule", replied Bobby. "Go get it," ordered Billy.

"Yes, we play in a tournament out there in two weeks. Why?" asked Bobby.

"Bobby, you won't believe this. So does my team", yelled Billy. "We will be playing against each other," Billy added.

"You've got to be kidding, Billy. What is the name of your team?" asked Bobby, not really believing his friend.

"We are the BA Yankees. That stands for Baseball Academy Yankees", answered Billy.

"Holy Smokes, we play you in the afternoon on Saturday," Bobby said with far too much excitement for the Skype line to handle. It crackled, and both boys started laughing, stomping their feet on the floor, and each could hear the other. Two best friends are getting to see each other after almost two years and playing against each other. What could be better?

After more than an hour of discussing their teams, their averages, their records and lawn mowing, Billy's Dad finally came in and told his son he had to get off Skype and get ready for bed.

"Didn't his Dad realize he wouldn't get any sleep tonight at all," thought Billy, as he told Bobby goodbye.

The team had two hard practices during the week, getting ready for their tournament in North Kansas City. There were different teams in different tournaments, although sometimes they played a team they had faced earlier. This tournament was one of those. The Wichita Shockers had come to North Kansas City this weekend. Coach Heier did not want to see the same results as before, when the Shockers shut them out, 10-0.

"Listen, guys, those players are good, but we can beat them," the coach preached to the team at both practices. After Thursday's practice, the coach huddled the team together once last time before the weekend tournament.

"We will be playing these guys our first game. All we have to do is win this one game, and we'll have a good chance of winning the tournament. I imagine John Gibbons, the pitcher we faced last time, will be throwing against us because their coach knows we didn't hit him at all", added Coach Heier.

"This time, we are going to wait for our pitch. I don't want any of you swinging at the first pitch. Get your eye on the ball from the moment it leaves his hand and wait. Just wait. If he gets behind in the count, he will throw his fastball over the center of the plate", added the coach.

He dismissed the team, telling them all to be there no later than 9:00 AM Saturday.

The next day at the game, Billy led off, and with more enthusiasm from the bench than in any other game, he singled and then stole second on the first pitch to Garrett. Garrett hit a grounder to the third baseman, and Billy had to hold at second. On the first pitch to Butch, Billy took off for third. He slid in, just as the ball got there, but he knew he was safe. The umpire motioned "safe," and the Shocker's manager came out to argue. Parents of the Shockers were in the stands yelling at the ump. Everyone on their side thought Billy was out, but he knew the ump wouldn't change his mind. Billy had watched major league baseball games and saw the instant replays, but in travel baseball, there was no instant replay, and if the ump said it was one way, it was. Billy was safe.

"Come on Butch, get me in," yelled Billy.

The bench was screaming, and Billy thought he heard one of the guys yelling to the pitcher. The parents of the Shockers were still yelling at the ump when Butch singled, scoring Billy. Will walked, and it was obvious, John Gibbons, the Shocker's pitcher was rattled. Tommy came up, let the first pitch go by as the Coach had instructed. "Ball one," yelled the ump. The Shocker parents were all screaming at the top of their lungs. This was a different type game than Billy had seen. Tommy let the count go to 3 & 2 before blasting a ball that cleared the left field fence, driving in Butch and Will. The Yankees led 4-0 in the first inning. The bench was going wild while the parents of the Shockers went deathly silent.

"Good game," Coach Heier told the team after they'd won 6-4.

Billy and Tommy turned two double plays, and Billy had two more hits, along with two more stolen bases. The Yankees won the tournament, by winning the afternoon game Saturday and the final game Sunday. After the last game, the coach started telling the team what to expect the following week.

"We are going to hold practice on Wednesday this week," barked Coach Heier. "Be there sharp because we have a lot of work to get done before leaving for Austin, and we will be facing teams down there that play all year long," Coach Heier added.

Billy wondered if that was true. "They play all year?" he asked his coach.

"Well, they don't play in December and January, but start playing games in February. Billy, we will be facing excellent teams", answered Coach Heier.

Billy thought about seeing and playing against Bobby. He was a lucky kid.

"Great games," Billy's Dad said on the way home. "I've got reservations for us in Austin next Thursday. We have to be at the airport two hours early, so be prepared to get up early", said his Dad.

All of a sudden, Billy realized he had lawns to mow that day.

"Dad, I've got four lawns to mow Thursday. What am I going to do?" Billy asked.

After much discussion, his Mom told him, "Billy, call your customers and tell those four that you will be moving their mowing up a day or two, and then you hustle and get all the yards mowed Monday, Tuesday, and Wednesday."

Billy thought that was a good idea, but he knew he'd be exhausted at Wednesday's practice. The youngster called his lawn mowing customers, explaining he would be mowing their lawn a day early and was surprised that he wasn't as tired as he expected after mowing all the yards by Wednesday.

It was a good practice and Billy Skyped Bobby that night.

"We are flying down on Southwest Airlines," said Billy.

"What time will you get here?" asked Bobby.

"Dad told me we are supposed to arrive at 4:30", Billy answered.

"Fantastic, Billy," replied Bobby.

He had already asked his Mom and Dad if they could take the Tankersly's to the Oasis that night for dinner, so as they got off the phone, both boys were jazzed to the point that there would be little sleep for either.

19

Together Again

All Billy could think about as they drove to the airport in North Kansas City was seeing Bobby and winning the games that weekend. He'd never flown before and was a little nervous about the flight, but nothing could take his mind off seeing Bobby. Billy was sitting between his Dad and Mom once they boarded the plane. He had to admit this was pretty exciting, but once in the air, he started to get bored. He decided to play a game with his Dad and Mom.

The Baseball Academy kept all his stats, and each week, the team would get a piece of paper that told them how they were doing as a team. They had just about every team stat you could think of, but Coach Heier also gave each player his own individual stats.

"Dad, what do you think my Batting Average is?" asked Billy.

".420 is my guess, Billy", his Dad answered. "Mom, what do you think?"

"I'd say you are hitting .565", she guessed.

"Mom is closest. I'm hitting .525", Billy informed them.

"How many bases do you think I've stolen?" Billy asked them both. Anything to pass the time the time until they landed.

"I think you've stolen...let's see...I think you've stolen 23 bases so far," chimed in his Dad.

"Too low," his Mom said. "33", she answered.

Billy said, "Dad wins that one. I've stolen 25 bases."

Before long, he heard the announcement over the intercom that they were flying over Wichita. He looked down and saw a city, but it was behind them almost as fast as it appeared.

"How fast are we flying," Billy asked.

"Probably around 550 mph", his Dad answered.

"Wow," exclaimed Billy, amazed that anything could go that fast.

Billy started reading a magazine, but couldn't keep his mind off seeing Bobby. Before long, he heard the flight attendant tell the people in the row in front of them that they were almost to Dallas. He leaned over his mother once again to look out the window. He could see a city in the distance. Billy kept staring out the window, and the city was getting bigger and bigger. He'd never seen a city that big.

"Dad, lean over and look at this city…it's Dallas, Texas", Billy told his Dad.

It didn't disappear like Wichita had, but stayed below them for a long, long time.

Billy was looking out the window, behind the plane and could still see Dallas as the Captain came on the Intercom, telling them they were ahead of schedule and would be landing in Austin in 30 minutes.

Billy's heart started beating faster. He was excited and nervous to see Bobby. He wondered if Bobby would look the same, and then realized that they'd been talking on Skype the night before and he hadn't changed a bit.

The 30 minutes passed slowly, but before he knew it, they were landing in Austin, Texas.

As they walked down the ramp to get into the main lobby of the airport, he was disappointed that Bobby was not right there at the gate.

"Where are they, Dad?" Bobby asked.

"Bobby's dad told me no one was allowed in the main part of the airport for security reasons, but they would meet us in the baggage claim area," his dad explained.

As they walked toward the baggage claim area, he saw and heard a band playing. There was a sign above them that said, "Austin, Texas, the live music capital of the world." Billy thought that was pretty cool, but he just wanted to see Bobby.

As they rode down the escalator, there was Bobby at the bottom. It was the longest escalator he'd ever been on, but once at the bottom, the two boys threw their arms around each other and hugged, while both were jumping up and down with excitement. Billy could not remember ever being this excited.

Bobby spoke first, "You've grown six inches, Billy."

"So have you," Billy responded.

His parents had decided on renting a car so Bobby's folks would not have to come to the hotel in the morning.

"Can I ride with Billy?" Bobby asked Mr. Banks as they walked to the car rental counter.

"Sure you can," answered his Dad and from that point on, all the boys could talk about was baseball and the tournament. They got their car, and before Billy even knew it, they arrived at the Hyatt Regency Hotel, which was the nicest hotel he'd ever seen.

Billy's Dad parked the car and John, and Sally Banks parked right next to them.

Once in the lobby, Mrs. Banks said to Billy's Mom, "Is this nice or what?".

"Amazing," said Julie Tankersly as they all decided to go check out the room.

The elevator was an all glass elevator that amazed Billy. Their room was on the 14th floor and looking down to the lobby of the hotel seemed like they were looking into the Grand Canyon, although Billy had only seen pictures of that. The elevator stopped, and they found Room 1412 that overlooked downtown and a lake.

Even Billy thought, "This is totally cool."

"Jim and Julie, we wanted to take you to the Oasis, a restaurant and club overlooking Lake Travis, but you guys have been traveling most the day, so let's just eat downtown and let the boys have some time together," spoke Mr. Banks.

"Sounds good to me," said Billy's father, while Billy's mother and Mrs. Banks were gabbing about something neither boy was interested in. All they wanted was to eat and talk about their games Saturday, and who was ahead in the money race of mowing yards.

They left the room, rode down the scary elevator again, and walked across the bridge, where hundreds of people were gathering on the Congress Avenue bridge.

"Austin is the bat capital of Texas," Mr. Banks said. "Millions of Mexican Freetail bats live under the bridge, and they come out at dusk to eat insects," explained Mr. Banks. "They are starting to fly out now. Look over the lake."

Billy looked, and it seemed like a cloud of smoke was coming out from under the bridge. There were so many of them. They just kept coming.

"Wow, that's pretty amazing," he said to Bobby.

"Wait until you see the ballpark, Billy," Bobby chimed in. Billy's mind left the bats immediately. He and Bobby started talking baseball again, as the group continued across the bridge.

"Do you remember Vince Young?" Bobby's Dad asked.

"Sure, he's the quarterback who won the National Championship for the Texas Longhorns several years ago," answered Billy's Dad.

"Well, that is where we are going to eat," said Mr. Banks.

As they entered the Vince Young Steakhouse, Billy had never seen anything that looked so expensive. Thankfully, Bobby's Dad said, "this is on us." Billy and Bobby both ordered the same thing, a filet minion steak since that's what the waitress suggested. But it was hard for the server to even to get their order as they were talking a million miles an hour about baseball.

20

Still Fastest

Dinner was over. The Tankersly's were back at the hotel, and it was agreed that Bobby was going to spend the night with them. Bobby told Billy about a "trail" along the lake and asked if he'd like to see it. Billy asked his Dad and Mom, and they confirmed with Mr. and Mrs. Banks that it was safe, so the two boys went running down the hall to the elevator.

A lady stopped them and said, "No running in the hotel, boys." They slowed down, got on the elevator and laughed at how high up they were and how scary it was riding that elevator.

Once in the lobby, Bobby said, "this way Billy." And they started running again. Outside, Bobby explained that the trail went for miles all around the lake.

They turned left, and Bobby said, "I'm faster than you now, Billy."

"No way," Billy shouted back as Bobby was saying, "OK, let's start here and race to that big tree."

"On your mark, get set, go," Billy shouted. It wasn't even close as Billy beat Bobby by 10 feet.

"Holy Smokes, you've gotten really fast, Billy," said Bobby in amazement. "How'd you do that?" he asked.

Billy explained about Mr. Booker, "who is in the Hall of Fame." He told Bobby how they ran together every day, how Mr. Booker was the one who gave him his metal spikes and got him into traveling baseball.

It was getting dark, and the boys returned to the hotel to find Billy's Dad and Mom, and the Banks sitting at the patio bar, called "Marker 10" or something like that. The boys really didn't pay attention to the name, all they were thinking about was baseball. Mr. and Mrs. Banks said they had to go, so after saying goodbye, the boys and Billy's parents rode up the elevator again. This time, it wasn't as scary for Billy and for the first time since arriving at the hotel, Billy spoke to his folks.

"This is a really nice hotel, Dad, and Mom. I've never seen a hotel this nice", he added.

Both Jim and Julie said the same, while Bobby was just happy they all were impressed with Austin. He had a secret plan of trying to get Billy to come live with him next summer so they could play together again.

21

Day Before

Friday was spent with the Banks family showing the Tankersly's much of Austin. Billy saw the LBJ Presidential Library and the Texas Longhorns baseball field that looked like a minor league park.

"The college kids play here?" he asked.

"Yep," said Bobby.

"This is where Coach Heier must have pitched in college," Billy pondered.

They saw SoCo, an acronym for South Congress Avenue, which was a unique shopping area near the hotel. They saw Mt. Bonnell, which had 102 steps to the top, overlooking Lake Austin. The 360-degree view was breathtaking and peaceful. Billy hadn't even thought of God recently, but he felt thankful to be with his best friend in Austin, and he actually heard himself saying, "Thank you, God." He learned that this had been a place Indians, and soldiers fought for Texas' Independence as far back as 1835.

Billy had to admit; the view was pretty cool as he could see for miles up a river that was called "Lake" Austin, for some reason Billy didn't understand because it looked like a river to him.

"This is nothing, Billy. Wait until we get to the Oasis", Bobby said excitedly before Billy could ask why a river was called a lake.

Their trip around Austin continued, and Mr. Banks told Billy's parents that "this little gas station is where Janis Joplin got her start."

Billy had no idea who Janis Joplin was but guessed she was a cook since it was now a restaurant. After driving up and down hills for what seemed like forever to Billy, they finally arrived at The Oasis, which was a restaurant on top of a cliff overlooking Lake Travis.

"Billy, you'll like this. Look down to the right. See those cliffs leading down to the water? That is known as Hippy Hollow, and they have legal nude sunbathing", said Bobby, as he peered that direction.

"Have you ever seen any girls down there?" Billy asked.

"No," Bobby answered, "but I keep looking every time we come out here!"

They both laughed and went back to their parent's table, overlooking the lake and the distant horizon.

They were seated up on the top deck and could see sailboats, speed boats, fishing boats, and a lot of multi-colored rafts in front of Hippy Hollow. Billy thought, "I wish Kansas City had something like this."

Bobby's Dad explained that at sunset, which would be in about 30 minutes, a bell would ring and people would start clapping as the sun went down. When it happened, it was funny to Billy because he could hear the clapping from the decks below. It was like one group would start clapping and then another. Finally, the sun was down completely, and the people on the top were finally clapping. Billy and Bobby joined in. That was fun.

After finishing dinner, they drove back to the hotel, and Mr. Banks told Bobby he had to come home with them.

"Come on, Dad," Bobby whimpered.

"You guys have a double header tomorrow, and you both need to get a good night's sleep, which you will not do if you stay down here," Mr. Banks uttered.

Both boys understood and wished each other luck in their game the next day as they left the Tankersly's room.

Billy was exhausted from the day's events and went right to sleep.

"It was good seeing the boys together again," stated Julie. Jim agreed and suggested they go downstairs for a drink before retiring. They sat on the patio, outside the Hyatt, right on LadyBird Lake, overlooking downtown.

"Austin sure did not remind me of the flat lands of Texas that we've read about," stated Jim.

"This is absolutely beautiful," Julie added.

"Now I know why they say Austin is in the Hill Country," Jim said.

Julie asked her husband if he'd gotten directions to the ballpark.

"Yes, and we need to leave about 8:00 AM to get there by 9:00 if there is traffic like we saw today", answered Jim.

They sat and talked for another 30 minutes before Julie said, "Jim, we need to get to bed because tomorrow is going to be a very long day."

22

Game Time

6:00 AM came early, but not early enough for Billy. He was up before his folks, thinking about playing against Bobby in the second game that day. Finally, his parents both got up. Billy's Mom spent what seemed like hours putting on makeup, and whatever a girl does, they went downstairs for breakfast.

Billy ate two pieces of bacon, one egg and said, "Ok, Mom and Dad, let's go."

"Are you a little excited, son?" Billy's Dad asked with a smile on his face.

They walked to their car and headed toward "Dell Diamond," where the Round Rock Express played.

On the way, they noticed a big complex of office buildings and Billy's Dad said, "That is where Dell Computers started, by a young guy who lived in Austin."

"Is the stadium named after them," Billy asked.

"I guess so," his Dad replied.

In another 15 minutes, they turned on the road pointing to the stadium. Billy really didn't know what to expect, but as they neared the stadium, he yelled, "There it is, Dad." They parked the car and headed inside where Coach Heier was already in the dugout. Billy put his spikes on, as he looked out over the field.

"Wow, Coach, we've never played in a park this beautiful," said Billy.

"Nope," answered the coach. "By the way, Billy," the coach said, as he turned toward the excited youngster. "I know you told me your best friend played on one of the teams in the tournament, but the schedule has been changed, and I'm not sure if we play them today or not."

Billy looked at the schedule change. His heart went down to his feet. They would not be playing Bobby's team today, and only if both teams won their two games would the two young friends get to play each other. Billy was devastated. He didn't want anyone to see him, so he went to the end of the dugout, with tears coming down his face.

He wondered if Bobby had heard the news yet. Bobby's team was playing their first game at the Texas Longhorns Park and then playing a night game after Billy's afternoon game at Dell Diamond. He made up his mind that the Yankees were going to win both games today if he had to get 10 hits. He just hoped Bobby's team won both of their games.

Coach Heier called the team together, telling them that this was like their World Series Tournament.

"Boys, even though we still have half a season to play, this is the longest trip we'll take, and we will be playing on mostly dirt infields from now on, not stadiums like this."

He continued, as they sat in the dugout, "This is a rare experience, and as I told you before, this is where the Texas Ranger's Triple A team, the Round Rock Express play. It is known as one of the nicest minor league parks in the nation. We need to win both games today to play for the Tournament Championship tomorrow. But, the teams we will be playing are mostly from the south, where they play baseball all year long, so we have our job cut out for us", Coach pointed out to the team.

When they took the field, they were the "home" team the first game, and Jack Hughes was pitching for them. Billy remembered how the Shockers had hit Jack all over the place in Wichita. He just hoped Jack had a better game today.

After striking out the side in the first inning, Billy was a little relieved and felt, "we can win this game." He came up and saw the coach give him the drag bunt sign.

He looked at the right field fence and thought, "I can hit it over that, and the coach wants me to bunt?"

"Strike One" the ump yelled after the first pitch. Billy was caught by surprise. It was a curve ball that dropped from his waist to his feet, and the ump called it a strike. He wanted to turn to the ump and say, "What?" but he kept his composure and resisted in letting the ump know what he thought of that call.

He also didn't want the pitcher to think he couldn't hit the curve, so he got in his regular stance, not indicating that he was going to bunt. The next pitch was another curve, but Billy was running toward first as his bat hit the ball before it curved.

"Safe" yelled the ump as Billy beat the throw. "Way to go, Billy," the guys in the dugout cheered.

On the first pitch, the coach gave Garrett the take sign, and Billy the steal sign. He edged off first base, was ready to run when the pitcher made a move he'd never seen and threw it to first. Billy dove back in safely and then didn't take quite as big a lead. Once it appeared to Billy that the pitcher's leg was over the pitching mound, Billy took off. The pitcher threw to first again, and Billy was halfway to second. By the time the first baseman threw to second, Billy slid in with another stolen base. Garrett still had not seen a pitch.

Finally, the pitcher for the PineRider's threw a strike to Garrett, but he'd been instructed to not swing at the first pitch, just wait for his pitch. Billy stayed at second, but he realized he could see the signs the catcher was giving the pitcher. He put down two fingers, which Billy figured meant another curve, and he took off for third base the second the ball was thrown. It was a ball, bouncing in the dirt, and Billy didn't even have to slide as there was no throw. Garrett dug in at the plate, determined to drive Billy home. After watching a couple of strikes called on him, he hit a hard grounder to third. Billy wanted to try to score but knew he'd probably be out. He stayed at third. Butch came up, hit another grounder to third, and Billy had to stay again.

With Will at-bat, Billy was sure he would get a hit. He was right behind Billy in hits for the season. "Strike one," the ump called. It was a fastball. Billy felt the next one would be a curve. He was ready to score if the ball got by the catcher.

It didn't happen. Will struck out, leaving Billy stranded at third. In the top of the second, Jack struck the side out again. Six straight strikeouts. Billy had never seen Jack pitch this good. By the time the 7th inning rolled around, the score was 2-1, in favor of the PineRiders. Billy was up second, and already had two hits, but he knew he had to get a hit this inning if there was any chance of playing Bobby's team on Sunday. Coach Heier decided to pinch hit for Jack, with Aaron Austin, a funny name to be playing in Austin. Aaron walked on four pitches.

Billy stepped in the batter's box knowing he needed to get a home run to win this game. He looked down the right field line. There was a short porch area for the fans that made the distance 300 feet instead of 330 feet for the regular fence. He knew he could hit it that far. On the first pitch, he swung with all his might.

"Strike one" yelled the ump. Billy stepped out of the batter's box, hit the clay off his spikes and stared at the pitcher. He knew he was going to get a fastball since had two hits on his curve.

As the team jumped up and down, Billy rounded the bases. He was as excited as could be. A home run, in the bottom of the 7th, to win the game. The Yankees still had a chance to play Bobby's team tomorrow. They needed one more win that afternoon.

The afternoon game had much less suspense as the Yankees scored 5 in the first inning, and marched on to a 9-2 win with Billy leading the team again. He had three hits, three stolen bases and scored three runs. Butch had a home run to drive Billy in during the Yankees first inning onslaught. The win meant that Billy would be playing Bobby's team if his team won the night game.

Bobby arrived in the third inning after the team's first game win. He and his Dad and Mom sat with Billy's Mom and Dad. Billy could hear them all cheering for him each time he came to the plate. He couldn't help it; he wanted to show off for Bobby.

His third time up, he wanted, in the worst way to hit one out of the Dell Diamond Stadium to show Bobby his new found power. He waited for his pitch and hit a hard line drive, but the right fielder cut it off in the gap and Billy couldn't even try for second, as he knew he'd be out.

After the game, Bobby was the first to greet him following the team meeting. "Great game, Billy," Bobby said, slapping him on the back. It felt so good to be back with his friend. It was like no time had passed at all.

The two boys ran off to get some food at one of the concessions stands and talked more about baseball. Billy was thrilled that Bobby was still into baseball as much as he was.

"Billy, you are not the only one who's been running," said Bobby. "I've been running a mile a day to try to get faster, but obviously, I'm not nearly as fast as you. I don't think any guy I've seen in the tournaments down here has been as fast as you", Bobby added.

"You know what's made the difference, Bobby?" asked Billy.

"No, what," asked Bobby, really wanting to know.

"My metal spikes," smiled Billy. "Do you remember how disappointed I was that first game when Coach Yam told us we couldn't wear metal spike?" asked Billy.

"Not really," responded Bobby.

"Dad and Mom had bought me a pair, and I still remember the ring of those spikes hitting the pavement that day. It was an amazing sound, and then Coach Yam said I had to change", explained Billy. "I wanted to quit right then. I went back to the car with Dad and cried like a little baby. Of course, I was only nine", laughed Billy. "But it was that day that I made up my mind I was going to be the fastest player ever and started working on my running, just waiting for the day I could wear metal spikes. When I found out we could wear them in travel baseball, I had no choice but to join the Yankees", said Billy.

"But what's made you so fast? You were down to second on your steal in the third inning before the catcher was even in a throwing position", Bobby asked and commented.

"I think the answer is Mr. Booker", said Billy.

"Who's Mr. Booker?" Bobby wanted to know.

"I told you about him last night. I guess you didn't hear me", Billy laughed.

"Hey, I was so excited to see you, Billy, I probably didn't hear half of what was said last night," Bobby was laughing too.

"Well, one day while running, this older man started running with me. I found out he was the only groundskeeper in the Hall of Fame along with Babe Ruth, George Brett, and all the rest. From what I heard, the reason he was elected was that he wasn't just a groundskeeper but a personal coach to many of the major league players. They would come to him for advice", explained Billy. "When he started working with me, I started improving my speed. He clocked me to first on a drag bunt that he said was faster than 90% of all the major leaguers", Billy told his friend, "And I want to be the fastest ever."

Bobby listened this time because he wanted to be as fast as Billy, although he had never been and probably never would be. His main strength was his power. He had 10 home runs so far this year and led his team. He was projected to hit 25 before the season was over, which would be about two months after Billy's team finished playing.

"Bobby, your coach is calling you," Bobby's Dad yelled out, halfway across the Stadium.

"Good luck in your game tonight, Bobby. You have to win you know", Billy said as Bobby was jumping over one seat after another to get down to the field.

Billy sat with the both boy's parents, and was impressed with Bobby's arm strength, but even more with his power. He threw two runners out trying to steal and hit a home run over the center field fence, which was 390 feet. "He has grown into a stud," thought Billy. Bobby's team won with the exact same score as the Yankees afternoon game, 9-2. That meant that at 1:00 PM tomorrow afternoon, Billy would be playing against Bobby. The boys jumped up and down together out in the parking lot after the game, and neither even thought to razz the other. As the two cars pulled out of the parking lot, both boys were leaning out the window yelling, "Bye" to the other. Billy slept well that night.

23

Hero?

Just as they had left Dell Diamond, at the same time the night before, both cars arrived at the same time for the Sunday afternoon game. The boys jumped out of their cars immediately talking to each other. Standing in the parking lot, Bobby told Billy that the pitcher for his team had thrown a one-hitter in his last game, and was really good.

"Bobby, our pitcher is Tom Wilhelm, and he throws a mean fastball, but his curve is all over the place," Billy told his friend.

"OK, Coach Heier is calling our team, Bobby. I have to go, but good luck today", shouted Billy as he ran through the parking lot, listening to his spikes hitting the parking lot surface. His only thought as he reached the dugout was, "We've got to win this game."

Bobby's team, the Giants, were the visitors and batted first. Bobby was hitting cleanup. Tom Wilhelm retired the side in order, so Bobby didn't get to bat in the first inning.

"Billy, I know you want to hit another home run to that short right field fence, but I want you to start off the game with a drag bunt again," Coach Heier told him while he was waiting for the warm up pitches to be over. Billy had actually come to like this drag bunt thing, especially since he'd never been thrown out when attempting it.

As Billy hit his spikes with his bat before getting into the batter box, and Bobby, who was catching, laughed at Billy. For the first time, Billy heard some razzing from his best friend.

"Do you really think that is going to help you get on base, batter?" Bobby said from behind his mask.

Billy looked at him and retorted, "Once I get on, I'll be stealing on the first pitch."

Bobby called for a curveball on the first pitch, remembering that Billy had a hard time even hitting a changeup back on the Rockets. With Bobby catching, Billy was sure he'd get a curveball on the first pitch, and he was ready. As soon as the ball left the pitcher's hand, Billy was running toward first with the bat almost thrown at the pitch.

Billy had noticed the third baseman was playing back while the first basemen had moved into the grass. Bobby's coach had seen or been told about Billy's drag bunting skills, so Billy laid the bunt down the third base line, and there wasn't even a throw to first. The Yankees were off the bench cheering Billy on. He was happy when he saw the third base coach give the steal sign on the first pitch.

Billy watched the pitcher in his stretch, and once again, he realized he was going to try to pick Billy off. The throw came, and Billy, who had not taken a big lead, almost walked back to the base standing up. "That was a lousy pickoff move," he thought to himself. On the first pitch to the plate, Billy ran.

He glanced back at Bobby, and that was just enough to let Bobby's throw beat him. He slid on the outside of the base, but the umpire raised his arm in the air indicating Billy was out. Billy was stunned. He'd never been thrown out trying to steal second. Once he got thrown out trying to steal third, but never second base. As he ran back to the bench, almost ashamed, his teammates encouraged him.

Garett and Butch both hit infield grounders and got thrown out, so the Yankees went scoreless in the last half of the inning, making it a 0-0 game after one inning.

On the way out to his position, Coach Heier stopped him, and said, "Billy, that was my fault. The catcher on the Giants called a pitch out, and you didn't have a chance", the coach told him. "We'll be smarter next time," added the coach as he jogged off the field.

Billy thought he should not have told Bobby, or shown him in their race that he was fast.

"Bobby outsmarted me on that one," Billy thought, and his mind went back to what Mr. Booker or Mr. Treehouse, he couldn't remember which, told him he had to play smart baseball.

"Hey batter," Billy yelled. "Look for a curve," he hoped to get even with Bobby for throwing him out because he knew that Tom's curveball was not very good. Then he remembered, he'd told Bobby about Tom's fastball. He called time and ran over to the mound.

"Tom, I assure you this guy will not be expecting a curve, but he can hit a fastball," Billy told his pitcher.

Tom shook off Jose's first sign, then the second, and finally, on the third sign, he nodded his head "yes." In came the curve and Billy was right, Bobby did not expect it, and swung wildly at a pitch, not even close to the plate. Billy smiled, but at the same time, felt a little sorry for Bobby because he'd been completely fooled. Tom threw three more curves, but

Bobby didn't swing, and all three were balls. It was pretty obvious; Tom had to throw a fastball on the next pitch, not wanting to walk the first batter of the inning. In came the fastball, and out it went, even faster than the pitch. Bobby had connected with the sweet part of his bat, and the Giants led, 1-0 as Bobby's homer looked like it was rising as it cleared the left field fence. As Bobby rounded second base, all Billy could do was say, "Nice hit, Catch." Bobby smiled at him, feeling happy that he'd homered against his best friend's team.

Billy came up again in the 4th inning. The third baseman and the first basemen were in on the grass, this time, expecting Billy to bunt again. He looked to his third base coach, hoping he would not give him a bunt sign again. He didn't. Bobby called for a fastball on the first pitch, hoping to surprise Billy. It did, but the ball was on the outside, and Billy knew to wait for his pitch. He fouled off the next two, so was behind in the count, 1-2. Billy knew Bobby would be calling for a curve, and he was ready, but the pitch bounced in front of the plate. "Ball two," shouted the ump. Bobby was talking to Billy the entire time.

"Hey batter, expect a curve again," teased the catcher. "You will not get hits down here in baseball land," razzed Bobby through his Catcher's mask. Billy was letting Bobby get to him, so he stepped out of the batter's box, hit his bat against his spikes, and told himself to focus. Stepping back in, he was determined to hit that porch in short right field. The pitch was a fastball over the plate, and the sound of the bat hitting the ball left no doubt. Billy had matched Bobby's home run, tying the game up. He circled the bases, excited to reach the plate to tell Bobby that players from the North could hit too. As he crossed the plate, instead of Billy saying anything, it was Bobby. "Nice hit, Billy," said his friend. Billy smiled without saying a word until the rest of the Yankees surrounded him, jumping up and down saying, "Great hit, Billy."

Bobby got another hit in the 4th but was left stranded. Billy didn't get up again until the 5th, and Bobby said, "Do not expect another fastball, Yankee." He wasn't referring to Billy's team name, but the fact that southerner's always called people from the north, Yankees. Billy watched four straight curveballs miss the plate, and he was on first without swinging the bat.

"Now, I've got to get a better jump to steal second," he thought. Coach Heier did not give the steal sign. Garrett took a curveball that was inside.

"No pitchout this time," the first base coach whispered to Billy in between pitches, "but this will be a fastball, so don't go." Sure enough, it was a fastball over the plate that Garrett swung and missed.

Billy was dying to steal second on his friend, but again, on the third pitch, the coach did not give him the sign to steal. Garrett let the ball go by without swinging, and it was inside again.

"Ball two," bellowed the ump.

Finally, on the 4th pitch, he got the sign he'd been waiting for. He took a little bigger lead, and the Giants pitcher noticed, so he threw over to first, not really trying to pick Billy off but letting him know he hadn't forgotten who was on first. On the next pitch, Billy was off running. The throw was, once again, a good one from Bobby, but Billy slid in safely. He turned and smiled at Bobby, but Bobby's back was to

Billy as he was picking up his mask that had sailed off his head as he threw as hard as he could to get his friend out.

On the very next pitch, Billy saw the pitcher go into his stretch, but the shortstop and second basemen were far off the bag, so Billy started running once the pitcher looked back to the plate. Bobby didn't even try to throw him out as he stole his second base of the day. Garrett hit a long fly ball to left, and Billy scored easily, making it a 2-1 game for the Yankees. Billy had scored both runs so far. This time, when Billy crossed the plate, Bobby didn't say anything because he was fielding a bad throw from the left fielder.

Bobby came up in the 7th, the last inning, with a man on first. Coach Heier walked out to the mound and signaled the left-handed Steve Folks to come in to relieve Tom. After Steve had thrown his warmups, Bobby stepped back in the batter's box, hoping to hit another home run to put the Giants in the lead, and hopefully win the game. After taking two straight balls on the outside, with one swing, Bobby showed everyone his power. The ball landed on the grassy berm behind the left field wall, giving the Giants a 3-2 lead. As Bobby rounded second base, all Billy could do was tip his hat to his best friend. Two home runs.

"Wow," thought Billy.

"You weren't kidding about developing power," Billy said to Bobby, as he was tipping his hat. Bobby just smiled.

It was the bottom of the seventh, and Billy wasn't going to be up until the fifth batter. He wanted one more chance to put the Yankees ahead. He dreamed of hitting a game-winning hit against his best friend's team, but he never got up, and the Giant's won, 3-2 on Bobby's two home runs. As the Giants celebrated, Coach Heier told his players that they'd played a good tournament.

"OK guys, we didn't win, but hopefully, we can schedule this trip again next year, because we are just as good as these southern teams, as we showed in our first two games. They may have gotten the best of us today, but we played excellent baseball. I'm proud of each of you", he concluded.

24

Learns a Secret

Billy had all sorts of emotions running through him. He was sad that they lost. He knew if he'd beaten Bobby's throw in the first inning, the game might be tied right now. At the same time, he was happy for Bobby. As the two met up at the cars in the parking lot, all Billy could do was congratulate his friend.

"Wow, Bobby, talk about winning the game by yourself," Billy muttered. "That was great, and as much as I hate losing, this might be the first time I haven't thrown my glove down after a loss," he told his friend. "I hate losing, Bobby."

Bobby smiled, a smile that only comes from winning.

Billy's parents had decided to stay one more night, and Bobby and his parents were coming down to the hotel for dinner. On the way to the hotel, Billy's Dad gave him some advice, which Billy really didn't want to hear. Bobby's team, and Bobby alone, had beaten the Yankees. Billy was in no mood for advice.

"Billy, do you know how Bobby threw you out in the first inning?" his Dad asked.

"Yes, Dad," Billy answered. "Bobby called a pitch out."

"No," his Dad started. "That was not the reason. The reason was you forgot to run straight to the base without looking. You took a quick glance back at Bobby, and that slowed you down just enough to let the second baseman put the tag on you", his Dad told him.

Billy realized what his Dad was telling him was the truth, and he made a note to himself to never do that again.

As they ate dinner at the Hyatt, Billy and Bobby talked about the game the entire time. Bobby confirmed what Billy's Dad had told him.

"Billy, I knew the second you looked back at me that I was going to get you," Bobby said.

"Yeah, Dad already got on me about that," said Billy.

"Where did all your power come from Bobby?" Billy asked.

"I've been lifting weights, and also, keep in mind, Billy, we get to play baseball all year long," Bobby replied. "That helps a lot," Bobby added.

"You really play all year long, Bobby?" asked Billy, knowing he heard Bobby say that yesterday, but it hadn't really sunk in until now.

"That's what I told you yesterday, Billy," Bobby declared, sort of disappointed that Billy hadn't really heard him the day before. "After all," thought Bobby, "that was going to be my main argument about why he should move down here and live with us."

Bobby thought this was a good time to bring up that idea.

"Billy, my folks, have said they would love to have you come down here and live with us for a year to be able to play ball the entire time," urged Bobby wanting his friend to think about it.

"Dad and Mom would never let me move down here, Bobby," replied Billy.

"They might if you asked," reassured Bobby.

Billy thought it was ridiculous to even ask.

After dinner, the boys walked around the Lake on the trail that went behind the hotel. They came to a place where a boardwalk jetted out over the lake, and they stood still for a minute or so, just looking at the Austin skyline. Billy had to admit; it was prettier than any he had seen. As they climbed up to the Congress Bridge, the Capital stood out, among the much taller and brighter buildings, reflecting off the lake.

"Bobby, you really did play a great game today," said Billy, finally getting over the loss. "I was proud of you, and as you rounded second base after your second home run, I saw you wink at me," said Billy. "To be honest, as much as I hate losing, I was happy for you."

Bobby repaid the compliment by telling Billy that he didn't doubt that Billy would steal more bases than anyone down south.

"If you hadn't looked back at me, you would have even stolen on my pitchout, and to be honest, that was the best throw I think I've ever made," smiled Bobby. If there was any bright side to losing to your best friend", maybe it was learning a lesson," thought Billy.

It was time to call it a night, and everyone hugged each other as the Banks car was brought to the front of the hotel. They had the Valet park their car earlier when returning from the game. The two best friends laughed, cried, and hugged each other goodbye, agreeing to keep talking on Skype. Billy was sad as he saw their car pull away.

25

Goals

After returning home, Billy's heart was just not into practice the first afternoon. As hard as he tried, he just could not get excited, or even "into the practice." His mind was still in Austin.

He'd talked to Bobby on Skype once getting home, and again, Bobby said, "you need to come down and live with me for a year so we can play together." That sounded so good to Billy.

Three more weekends passed with the Yankees winning all their games. Billy got one hit after another and stole one base after another. After playing at the 3&2 Stadium in Kansas City, Missouri one afternoon, a scout for the St. Louis Cardinals talked to Billy, telling him he had a lot of potential and he would be following the youngster.

Before he knew it, the season was almost over. It was starting to get cold in Kansas City, but there was one more tournament in Harrisburg, Missouri. The Yankees won the first two games, and Coach Heier encouraged the team to play their best game of the season in the final. They did, winning 6-5 with Billy scoring four runs. He'd been on base each time up and stole three bases, to set a new record for traveling baseball in the Midwest. It had been a good year for Billy and for the team.

The season was over, and Billy started running with Mr. Booker again. They talked and talked and talked as they ran. Mr. Booker's son had recovered and was doing well. His car had been hit by four teenagers who had been drinking. They ran a red light, broadsiding Mr. Booker's son's car. Billy made a mental note never to drink and drive and never run a red light. It would have been sad if Mr. Booker had lost his son.

As the days went on, Billy listened intently as Mr. Booker told him what he saw in the games. Some of the things were good; some were things Mr. Booker thought he could improve. Billy was learning. But he still missed Bobby.

When he got home, Billy called Bobby, but there was no answer. He sat down at the table for dinner. His Mom had something in the oven that smelled great.

"What is that Mom?" he asked. His Mom told him what all was in the dish she'd prepared, but Billy's mind was on Bobby.

"Why hadn't he answered?" Billy thought.

The family had a good time at dinner as his Dad talked about the upcoming basketball season.

At one point, Billy asked, "Does KU have a football team, Dad?"

The mood at the table changed immediately.

"Billy, KU used to have a good football team, but lately, we haven't done very well," his Dad started. For the next five minutes, the discussion was on what the KU football team had to do to improve. Billy thought his dad should have been a KU coach. All of a sudden, his Dad stopped talking about the football team and started talking about the basketball team again. The mood was light-hearted, with a lot of laughter as his Dad told stories about KU basketball teams of the past.

The second Billy found a place to excuse himself, he did, running to his computer to Skype Bobby. Still no answer. Billy decided to check out his Facebook page as he had not even looked at it for a month. He belonged to a group for the Kansas City Royals, so he immediately went to read about the Royals. It was almost time for the Winter Meetings, and supposedly, one of the players with the Royals was a Free Agent, and other teams were willing to pay more than the Royals. No one knew what would happen, but the Royals fans were hoping the team would resign him. Then, one blog talked about the speed of Taylor Warren, a minor league outfielder for the Royals who stole 65 bases last year.

"That guy must be fast," Billy thought. He googled him and found out this was his third year in the minors. Then he watched a video by a local newscaster about Warren.

"Taylor Warren has spent three years in the minors and has more stolen bases than anyone in the history of minor league baseball in his first three years. So why haven't the Royals promoted him? Mainly because he has not shown, he can hit minor league pitching. If he got on more, he'd break the Majors stolen base record, but for now, Warren lingers at Omaha, hoping he can find magic in his bat."

The video ended, but Billy thought a lot about it.

"So what if I'm fast. If I can't hit for a high average, I won't even make the majors", Billy thought.

He decided he needed to get a pitching machine to start hitting every day. But, soon it would snow. He hated winter. It got in the way of him playing baseball.

"Bobby, thankfully, you answered. Where were you?" Billy asked.

"We had practice tonight. This weekend, we are playing the Waco Warriors at Waco.

"I am so jealous, Bobby. I wish like everything I could be down there", said Billy.

"Hey, you know my folks told me you could live with us, so it's your own fault you are not playing right now," chided Bobby.

"It's already cold up here, Bobby, and all I can do is run. Have you heard of Taylor Warren?" Billy asked.

"No," Bobby replied as he googled Taylor Warren. "I just googled him, Billy. He seems fast", said Bobby. Billy looked at his friend on his computer screen and explained that he wasn't in the majors because he couldn't hit.

"Bobby, I need to improve my hitting if I want to set a major league record for steals," Billy complained and hoped at the same time.

"Are you still thinking you are going to set a major league record for stolen bases? Geezzz, that's what you said back when we were on the Rockets together", laughed Bobby.

"I am," said Billy, "as a matter of fact." But, how am I going to learn to hit better?", asked Billy. Bobby had the answer for that right away.

"You need to practice more. You need to face more pitchers. You need to live in Austin", announced Bobby cheerfully.

That made Billy more depressed, and after they had hung up, he laid on his bed staring at the ceiling thinking about how he was going to get more practice in game situations. He'd heard that some of the guys who played traveling baseball were on two teams at the same time. He finally went to sleep, thinking of having a bat in his hand.

Billy spent the winter exercising in his basement on the equipment his Dad had bought him. He was growing by leaps and bounds and was now 5'10' and weighed 175. He and his Dad talked about baseball or practiced on most days until Christmas passed and his birthday was only a week away.

It was snowing on his 14th birthday. All he could think about was, "how fast will this melt?" He decided to have "that" talk with his Dad about moving to Austin.

26

Major Decision

"Dad, if I'm going to make the Majors, I'm going to have to learn to hit better," began Billy talking to his Dad.

"OK, I know you've got something on your mind. Spill it", directed Billy's Dad.

"Well, I need to get more practice, more than I'm getting here," nervously beginning to lay out his idea. "You know, Bobby's folks have invited me to come live down there, where I could play games from March to November, and get more practice to improve my hitting," continued Billy.

"No Billy. You just turned 14 years old. Talk to me two years from now, and I might think about it, but not now", Billy's Dad said emphatically.

"There's something else I want to talk to you about, Billy, "his Dad changed subjects. "Do you realize that you can't even be drafted until you've graduated from high school?"

"No, I didn't know that, but I do know the Royals have signed 16-year-old kids", said Billy, trying to wrap his mind around his Dad's statement.

"Yes, Billy, the Royals can sign kids from other countries when they are 16, but for whatever reason, the same rules don't apply here. You have to graduate from high school before any team can draft you", explained his Dad.

"Well, OK, I've got to figure out a way to graduate a year early. I'll be a sophomore next year, but maybe if I can take more classes, I can graduate a year early", thought Billy, immediately. He had a goal.

"Billy, I know you want to play in the majors, and you might be good enough for some team to put you way down on their draft list at 16 if you graduated early. However, if you wait until you are 17 and have graduated, there is a chance you could be a first or second round pick", advised his Dad.

"Dad, I know I have to improve my hitting," Billy said. "I've told you since I was 9 years old that I was going to set a record for stolen bases in the major leagues, but if I can't hit major league pitching, I'll never make it to the majors. I've got to get more practice against real pitchers. I wonder if I lived with Bobby and went to school there if I could take enough classes to graduate early?" Billy asked, ignoring the advice his Dad had just given him.

"Billy, here's the deal. If you can figure all that out, and really see you could graduate early, I will consider you going to Austin to get more practice....next year. The answer is a definite 'no' now", his Dad said firmly, believing that this was a spur of the moment thought-process from his son that would be forgotten by next year.

Billy hated to admit it, but his Dad was probably right, but he needed more hitting practice. How was he going to get that at the Baseball Academy? He knew he would get some, but not like playing real ball in Austin. "I'm going to see if I can get some advice on how to graduate early," he thought.

Monday morning, Billy didn't just call the school, he ran through the snow to school to talk to his counselor. He arrived early enough to speak to Miss Eye.

"Miss Eye," he started. "I want to graduate a year early, what do I have to do?" Miss Eye said it was possible but would require a lot of extra work with extra classes.

"Miss Eye, what if I transfer to another school after this year?" Billy continued.

"Billy, I would warn you against trying to graduate before your class, unless you have a good reason," Miss Eye explained to Billy. "As far as transferring to another school, they would have to approve all your classes here, in order to graduate early, which is another obstacle you'd have," continued his counselor.

"Well, it could be a very good reason, but I won't know that until after I graduate," said Billy, not really knowing what to tell her.

"What is the mystery?" she asked.

Billy looked at her, not knowing whether to explain it all or not. He felt she might think he was nuts. Miss Eye was a young woman, who Billy thought, might be a baseball fan.

"Are you a baseball fan," he asked.

"Absolutely, Billy. I go to Royals games all the time." Billy paused, not knowing if he should tell her why he wanted to graduate early.

"Miss Eye, I'm a good baseball player, but major league teams cannot sign anyone in the states until they've graduated from high school. If I lived in a different country, I could be signed at 16, but not here unless I've already graduated from high school", Billy explained to her.

"Billy, what if you graduate early and then don't get signed, what are your plans then?" she asked. "I don't know, Miss Eye," confessed Billy.

Billy left Miss Eye's office, more confused than before.

"What if I don't get signed," he thought, as he tried to pay attention in class. After school, Mr. Booker appeared out of thin air and was running with him.

"What's up, Billy?" he asked as he kept pace stride for stride.

"Hi, Mr. Booker. I went in early today to talk to my high school counselor, trying to find out how I could graduate early", Billy told his running advisor.

After about 100 yards or so, Mr. Booker said, "You think you might get signed, and know that you have to graduate from high school first, right?"

Billy stopped running.

"Yes, Mr. Booker", Billy muttered.

"OK, Billy, what happens if you don't get signed after working so hard to graduate in three years?" Mr. Booker asked.

"That's the same question Miss Eye asked me," Billy sighed.

"Well, did you give her an answer?" the man asked.

"No, because I don't have one," Billy admitted.

As they started running again, Mr. Booker told Billy that a scout for the Royals had talked to him about the 14-year-old.

"He said the Royals are still watching you," Mr. Booker explained to Billy, excited to give him encouragement to keep working hard.

"Really," Billy stopped again.

"Yes, but that doesn't mean they are ready to sign you. It does suggest that you probably have a chance to get drafted at some point, but probably not when you are 16", stated Mr. Booker. "Personally, I'd stay in school, play with the traveling team since your tuition is already paid, graduate with your class, and practice constantly until then," he continued.

Billy had not mentioned that he might want to move to Austin, even though right now, his dream was semi-fading. When they reached Billy's home, Mr. Booker asked if Billy was going to run with him on days that he wasn't practicing with the Yankees. Billy told him that would be great as he waved goodbye to Mr. Booker, who looked older than the last time they ran together. Billy even noticed Mr. Booker was out of breath by the time they reached his home.

The next day, Billy arranged with Miss Eye to take more classes next fall, even though she thought he would probably change his mind.

After dinner, Billy Skyped Bobby, just to talk, but Bobby didn't answer.

"He's probably got a game," thought Billy, discouraged that his plan was not going as he hoped.

The next day, he called Coach Heier to ask when practice for the new season would start and found out that it would not start as early as it had in the past years because Mr. Elton was reorganizing the Academy.

"What's he doing?" Billy asked.

"Well, Billy, after the Yankees played in Austin, I explained to Mr. Elton that our boys were not getting to play as many real games as the kids in the south", Coach Heier began. "He's trying to figure a way for all the teams at the Academy to get more games and has come up with an idea, but I don't know what it is," the Coach told Billy.

Billy and Mr. Booker ran together for a week, talking about what Mr. Elton was going to do for the Academy, as Billy knew Mr. Booker and Mr. Elton were good friends. He found out that Mr. Booker and Mr. Elton had discussed a plan, but Mr. Booker wouldn't tell Billy what it was.

27

Big Announcement

A week later, his parents received a letter from the Baseball Academy.

"What does it say," asked Billy, wondering if the Academy was going out of business or something? He had no idea. Because Mr. Booker did not sound excited when he told Billy there was going to be some type of change, he had all sorts of negative thoughts running through his mind.

Dear Baseball Academy Parents:

The Baseball Academy of Leawood has determined our boys are not receiving the benefit of playing games as early as the teams in the South, keeping them from attaining their full potential. When discussing this with Mr. Holister Ostoff, head of the non-profit Leawood Sports Association, he got excited about helping local youth. He took his idea to his Board of Directors, and they voted to pay all expenses for a week-long trip to Surprise, Arizona during Spring Training for one of the Baseball Academy teams and their parents each year. This year's team will be the Yankees. Next year will be the team from the Academy that finishes with the best record. This is during Spring Break so the boys will not miss school.

Coach Heier of the Yankees, working with Mr. Ostoff and several major league GM's, arranged a tournament with traveling teams from the south. Games will be played at various major league Spring

Training camps when the major league teams are not playing at their home field. There will be eight games, in a round robin tournament, played from March 12th through March 18th.

Practice for all the Academy teams will begin at the Academy on February 15th.

A schedule will be released by March 1st for the tournament in Phoenix. Yankee players and parents will be staying at the Hyatt Place hotel. (See attached map) The hotel rooms will be reserved in your name starting March 11th to March 20th, allowing the boys to see two major league Spring Training games after they have completed the tournament.

To Yankee parents: Please respond to the attached letter to confirm you and your son (s) will be able to make this trip.

Sincerely,

John Elton
Baseball Academy of Leawood.

"You still want to move to Austin?" Billy's Dad laughed out loud. Coach Heier had already run this by the parents, but nothing was definite until the official letter arrived.

"Dad, is this real?" Billy asked being totally shocked.

"We get to play games in March, at the Royals training site?" said Billy with a question in his voice.

"Well, the team does, Billy, but that's when March Madness is on, so we won't be able to make it," said his Dad.

This shocked Billy even more.

"Dad, they will have TV sets out there," said Billy, wondering if his Dad would really rather watch KU basketball games than see his son play at the Royals Spring Training camp.

"Billy, I'm teasing you. Mom and I wouldn't miss this for anything", replied Billy's Dad.

With that, Billy was headed straight toward his computer to Skype Bobby.

"Bobby, you won't believe what I'm about to tell you," said Billy, once Bobby had answered.

"You always start our Skype calls that way," laughed Bobby. "What, Billy?" he asked.

"Our team is going to get to go to Phoenix this spring and play games for a full week at the Royals Spring Training Camp," screeched Billy into his headset.

"No way," said Bobby.

"Yes way," replied Billy as he got the letter from Mr. Kelly and read it to Bobby.

"Now, I'm the one who's jealous, Billy," said Bobby. "Gezzzz, you are getting to play games almost as early as we are."

The two 14-year-old boys had talked for over an hour before Bobby said his folks were telling him he had to get off. Billy was disappointed as he could have talked for another hour.

28

Practice Makes Perfect

The first practice for the Yankees was getting to know the new guys and a little hitting practice. Billy really liked one of the new kids on the team. He was a catcher by the name was Cameron. Billy didn't know his last name, but after seeing him catch batting practice, and watching him hit, Billy felt he would be starting by the time they got to Phoenix.

"Hey Cam, where do you go to school?" Billy asked.

"I'm from Lawrence. I'm sorry, but I forgot your name", Cameron replied.

"Billy Tankersly," said Billy as they left the building.

Mr. Booker was waiting for Billy, so he didn't have much time to talk to Cameron.

"Billy, how did the first practice go?" asked Mr. Booker as they ran the three blocks to Billy's home.

"Nothing particular, Mr. Booker. We just did a little hitting, and spent time meeting the new guys", answered Billy.

"Any new guys who will get to start this year?" asked Mr. Booker.

"Maybe one. His name is Cameron something or other. I didn't get his last name, but he lives in Lawrence", added Billy.

He's a catcher, and looked pretty good", Billy said.

By now, they were at the Tankersly home and once again, Billy noticed that Mr. Booker was out of breath.

"You feeling OK?" Billy asked.

"Yes, the doctors say I have something called COPD. It at least got me to quit smoking", said Mr. Booker. Billy looked at him wondering when he ever smoked. Billy never saw him with a cigarette.

"I've never seen you smoke, Mr. Booker", commented Billy, looking at the graying man.

"That's because I never let you or anyone else see me," smiled Billy's running friend.

They waved goodbye, and Billy was anxious to tell his Dad and Mom about the new kid on the team and to talk more about the Spring Training trip. He had an idea.

"Dad and Mom," Billy started. "What would you think about having Bobby come over to Phoenix while we are there?" he quizzed them.

"Billy," his Dad spoke up. "You and Bobby will be best friends forever, but there are some things you have to do by yourself. Do you realize that there will be major league scouts watching you play in Phoenix?" he quizzed his son.

"No, no one told me that," said Billy with wide eyes.

"Well, think about it, Billy," his Dad said in a lecturing manner. "This is Spring Training, and more than half the teams in the majors have their training in Phoenix, including the Royals. Do you think these scouts who are always looking for talent will not be at your games?" Jim Tankersly asked his son. "In fact, son, major league teams have been cutting down on having scouts because of all the metrics available to the teams," his Dad continued, "So this will be one of your best chances actually to have more scouts see you play."

"Dad is right," thought Billy. "I should have realized that," but he did not know major league teams were cutting back on their scouting programs.

"Dad, forget my idea about Bobby. I want to play the best I can with no distractions", Billy acknowledged his Dad's comment without admitting he should have thought about it.

That night, Billy worked out harder than he had in weeks. He even spit-shined the new metal spikes that his Dad and Mom had given him for his birthday.

His mind for the next three weeks was on nothing but playing good baseball in Phoenix. Every practice to him was like a game. Finally, practice was over, and it was time to fly to the Royals spring training camp.

29

Agents and Scouts

When they got to the airport, it was like the entire team was taking the same flight. The parents switched seats to let the boys be together, and Cameron sat next to Billy. They talked the entire 2 ½ hour flight about getting to play in front of scouts.

Billy had found out over the last three weeks that Cameron was an excellent baseball player. He had an arm that was equal to Billy's, and baserunners would be foolish to try to steal on him. Once they arrived, several of the parents agreed to meet at a restaurant that one of the parents had eaten at years ago, but Billy wanted to go straight to the hotel, and get sleep.

Hyatt Place was a suite hotel that had a living room, kitchen, and bedroom. Billy slept on the couch that night while his folks stayed in the bedroom. As hard as he tried to go to sleep, it seemed impossible. He really didn't know what time he finally got to sleep, but it didn't take an alarm to get him up. He realized he was nervous, not something that he usually experienced.

"Billy, how are you feeling?" his Mom asked as she came out of the bedroom in a white bathrobe he'd never seen.

"Mom, I'm sorta nervous," he admitted. Normally, it was his Dad who gave him a pep talk, but this morning, it was his Mom.

"Billy, I normally let your Dad talk to you about baseball, but you have no reason to be nervous. You, my son, are a very gifted baseball player. You have talent, and all the tools I keep hearing about. In the grandstands, I hear the other parents telling me what a great young player you are. Each game, I leave very proud of you, and today will be no different", his Mom spoke to him in a very confident manner.

That helped Billy relax, and after a good breakfast, they were on their way to Surprise, Arizona, about 20 miles from the hotel. He wondered if he'd see any of the Royals. He wondered how good the team they were playing first would be. He wondered about a million other things before pulling into the Royals Spring Training camp. It looked just like the pictures on the Internet. There was the stadium that seated more than 10,000 people, along with six practice fields. The entire camp was shared with the Texas Rangers.

"Boys, we are playing in the Stadium today because the Royals and Rangers are playing at other fields around Phoenix. You will notice players on the practice fields. These are the guys from the Royals and Rangers who didn't go to their particular games so you may have some major and minor leaguers stopping their practice to watch you play. Pretty exciting", exclaimed the coach, who seemed to be as excited as the boys.

They all looked out over the complex and saw many players there on the different fields, and it was only 9:00 AM. Billy was impressed at their dedication as he got to watch a little of the batting practice on field three, which he believed to be the Rangers minor leaguers and maybe a few of the players on the Rangers 40 man roster. Even though it was batting practice, it seemed most were strong as they hit one ball out of the park after another.

Coach Heier spoke up to the team. "Guys, we are playing the Tucson Tornadoes in our first game. I don't know anything about them, so we are all going to be learning this first game about how good our competition is", stated the coach.

The team learned real fast that their competition was going to be stiff, but beatable. The Yankees were leading 6-2 after the 6th inning when Coach Heier put in the subs, knowing that 8 games were going to wear the boys out. Billy had walked and had hit a long HR before his time to bat in the 6th arrived.

"No stolen bases this game," thought Billy.

But his long HR over the right field fence attracted the attention of a couple of scouts. Billy's Dad overheard two of them talking about Billy, who gave him high marks in the way he played defense and his potential power.

When Jim Tankersly told Billy that, his response was, "they haven't even seen me steal yet."

The second and third games were easy wins for the Yankees, who were building more and more confidence. Billy did steal three bases in the two games, and hit another HR, just barely clearing the right field fence. He wondered how many scouts saw him steal those bases.

The second game had been played at Hohokam Stadium in Mesa, Arizona, home of the Oakland Athletics, while the third game was played at Tempe Diablo Stadium, home of the Los Angeles Angels. Billy figured most the people in the grandstands were parents or scouts, but so far, no one had come up to him.

What he did not know was that four different scouts had talked to his Dad and Mom during the game. They all wanted to know more about Billy. They asked all sorts of questions, such as, "was Billy planning on going to college, or junior college?"

They explained to Mr. and Mrs. Tankersly that Billy could not be drafted until after four years if he went to a four-year university, but after his freshman year if he went to a Junior College. They explained about the drafting system, and many things Billy's parents needed to learn about their son's potential future in professional baseball. The scouts all thought that was a possibility.

Back at the hotel, Billy was jazzed as was everyone else after their last win.

"Hey, Cam, we play back at the Royals camp tomorrow," stated Billy over dinner. "It's an afternoon game, and I'm hoping we get to see some Royals," he said.

"Did you see Dick Swazzer today?" asked Cam.

"No, you saw him?" questioned Billy jealously.

"I'm pretty sure it was him. He's big", replied Cam. "Who is your favorite Royals players, Billy?" Cam asked.

"I've got two favorites. Hos and Moose", smiled Billy. "Who is your favorite?" he asked Cam.

"No doubt, it's Salvy," answered Cam, since Salvy was the catcher for the Royals.

"Should have guessed," laughed Billy.

When dinner was over, the boys went swimming in the indoor pool and were thrashing in the water when Billy hit his head on the side of the pool. He wasn't hurt, but sank to the bottom, playing a trick on Cameron.

"Billy," screamed Cameron, "are you OK?"

Billy came up laughing, which sort of made Cam mad, but he laughed along with Billy, thinking, "I'm going to get even with him one of these days." Cameron had already learned that Billy was a practical joker, even in the three weeks of practice, and he liked that about Billy.

The afternoon game at the Royals camp was sort of a disappointment as they had to play on one of the practice fields because the Royals were playing in the Stadium. Billy figured all the scouts would be at the Royals game but was surprised after the game that a man came up to him, introducing himself as a scout for the Oakland A's.

"Billy, I saw you play at Mesa and today. I was very impressed with your defense, your power, and your speed", said the scout, who introduced himself as Mark Thompson.

"Thank you, Mr. Thompson", said Billy, looking closely at the man to see if he could be the Mark Thompson who used to play for the Cardinals.

"Billy, you are what, 14 years old?" asked Mr. Thompson.

"Yes sir," answered Billy, starting to get a little more comfortable with a scout talking to him.

"Do you have an agent yet?" the man asked.

"What?" Billy thought as he replied that he did not.

"Well, Billy, I'd suggest you start thinking that direction because after what I saw, you will get drafted once you finish high school," said Mr. Thompson, without a smile. "I'll be in touch," concluded the man.

Billy thought that had to be the best news he could have possibly heard, and he could hardly wait to tell his Dad and Mom.

Little did he know that the other scouts that had previously talked to his Dad and Mom suggested that they not hire an agent until after he was drafted. When Billy told them about the Athletics scout, and what he had said about an agent, Mr. and Mrs. Tankersly questioned amongst themselves if the man Billy talked to was really an agent, rather than a scout.

30

Back to Reality

He felt this had been the best week of his life. He stole a total of 8 bases in the eight games, and had two home runs, as well as getting 15 hits. He also made two spectacular plays where he was able to show his speed on defense and his arm strength.

Everyone stayed to watch the Royals play two games after the tournament was over. Billy got the courage to go down to the seats behind the dugout to get autographs. It was the wrong time of practice for the players to come over to the grandstands, so he came up empty-handed, but got close enough that he recognized most of the Royals. All through the game, Billy was studying Esky, the shortstop for the Royals. He was learning, just by watching intently. He made up his mind; he wanted Coach Heier to hit more grounders to his right during infield practice when they got home.

The trip came to an end, with Cameron sitting next to Billy on the flight back. The boys talked about the entire week. Cameron had thrown out three runners, who tried to steal on him. No one else even tried, as word got out about Cameron's strong arm. He also had 12 hits with one home run. Both boys were proud of the other.

Back in Kansas City, the weather had turned bad with a late season snow storm. As the plane landed, Billy could see ice plows cleaning the runway, and was thankful they landed safely. On the drive home, Jim and Julie reviewed the week with Billy. At one point, Billy asked his Dad if he should get an agent, and Jim Tankersly gave the same response as he had about Billy moving to Austin.

"Keep improving, Billy, and we will when the time is right," said his Dad.

Mr. Booker met Billy after school the first day back, wanting to know what had happened in Phoenix.

"Mr. Booker, I had a scout tell me I had potential", started Billy, telling him about the week.

"Billy, you have really grown the past year. I think many scouts are going to talk to you in the next two years. "I know your Dad said you should not get an agent yet, and I agree with him," stated Mr. Booker. "But, I don't think it would hurt for you to talk to an agent."

"I wouldn't even know where to look to find an agent, and aren't you suppose to get a good agent who will get you the best terms and money?" asked Billy.

"Let me talk to a friend of mine and see what he says," Mr. Booker ended the conversation as they got to Billy's home.

Billy had not Skyped Bobby all the time in Phoenix. He was too tired when they had gotten home. He had school the next day, so it was that night when Billy finally Skyped his friend.

"Bobby, you won't believe what a great trip we had," Billy starting reliving the week with Bobby. After more than an hour on the phone, Billy said he had to go to dinner. He did tell Bobby about the Scout but didn't go into it other than to say the scout told him he had potential.

Practice that week was hard. All the boys still had their heads in Phoenix. Coach Heier informed them that they would be playing their first games back home in three weeks if it didn't snow again. All of a sudden, it got warm like it did so many spring days in KC, but everyone knew it could get cold again real fast.

The games that summer went by quickly. The Yankees definitely had the best team in the Midwest. They won three straight tournaments. Billy had four home runs. He was seeing how the exercising in the basement was paying off. He was much stronger, and faster as well. He stole four bases, which was his low this far into the season, but Coach Heier didn't give him the steal sign as much, because Cameron was showing off his power as well, hitting six home runs.

"Cameron, do you work out at all in Lawrence?" asked Billy after their last tournament game.

"Absolutely," said Cameron. "I want to play pro ball, and have spent the last three years working out on exercise equipment my Dad bought for me."

Billy started laughing. He knew he and Cameron were a lot alike, but he had no idea that Cameron worked out like he did. But, Cameron's comments made Billy even more determined to work out more, without sacrificing his running with Mr. Booker each day there was not practice.

The summer was almost over before Billy even realized it. The Yankees were 32-4 in their 36 games, not counting their seven wins in Phoenix. It was time for the last two tournaments of the year, meaning that even though they got to start sooner, they were not going to get in the 60 games that they'd played last year.

They only won two out of three games in their next to the last tournament, losing by one run to the Manhattan Broncos. Billy had another good game but grounded out in his final at-bat. Once again, a single would have won it, but Billy was swinging for the fences with his new found power. On the way home, his Dad brought that up.

"Billy, it seems to me I remember another game where you would have won if you had not swung for a home run on the last pitch," Mr. Tankersly said to his son. Billy had never forgotten his championship game where he struck out with the tying run on third.

"Dad, you are right," frowned Billy, just thinking about the game with the Rockets. "I remember telling you that I'd learned my lesson, but apparently not, "Billy added, kicking himself once again for swinging so hard that he had fallen to his knees.

"Well, it is a little different this year, Billy," his Dad commented. "You are much stronger and have been hitting home runs all year. How many do you have so far?" asked his Father.

Billy laughed. His Dad knew exactly how many home runs his son had hit.

"25", he replied.

"I've really been proud of you, son, for all the hard work you've put into getting better," Billy's Dad explained. "But, remember, you've got to play smart baseball as well, and a single that last game would have tied it up."

"I know, Dad," Billy answered, shaking his head. He began thinking about the last tournament of the year, which was going to be played in Gardner, Kansas. He wasn't going to make the same mistake and vowed to play "smart ball" from now on.

31

Mom's Advice

The Yankees won the tournament, and the season finished on a high note after they won all three games. He was going to be a sophomore and would turn 15 years old right after the first of the year. When school started, he enrolled in his extra classes. He knew his schedule would be hard, but with additional classes for four straight semesters, Billy was confident he could get enough hours to graduate in time for the June draft after he turned 16.

The team was still practicing at the Academy once a week, and Mr. Booker was running with Billy almost every night except when there was practice.

"Billy," Mr. Booker started, as they ran a different way home. "I've talked to Mr. Ward, a scout for the Royals, who has followed you all year. He tells me that next year when you graduate if you graduate early, there is a good chance the Royals will draft you in June. Obviously, he had no idea which round because that would be determined by the improvement you show next year."

"Really," Billy said excitedly.

"Yes, and I have talked to an agent friend of mine, who said he would be glad to speak with you to answer any questions you have," Mr. Booker said, almost as excited as Billy.

"Wow, that would be so great, Mr. Booker", yelled Billy, over the noise of the traffic.

When they reached Billy's home, they said their goodbyes, and as usual, the first person he wanted to tell this news was his Dad. But, his Dad was on a business trip that had taken him out of town, so he told his Mom. She took a cautious approach to everything. She was happy for him but warned him about something that had happened in his life.

Billy now had a girlfriend from school. Her name was Abigale. They both laughed a lot together. He got to take her out on a double date one weekend with Cameron and his girlfriend, Monica. The boys took their dates out to dinner and then to a movie in Lawrence. Cam was driving, and Billy didn't get home until after midnight. When he walked in the front door, he saw his Mom still up, sitting in the living room. He figured she was going to get on him about staying out so late.

"Billy, girls, can sometimes take up so much of your time, that you will forget to keep exercising," his Mom warned.

"That will not happen, Mom. I am going to play major league baseball, and nothing will stop me", said Billy, giving his Mom more confidence that Billy was not getting in over his head with Abigale.

But, it did get Billy to thinking. He realized his mind had been on Abigale more than baseball the past few weeks. Christmas was coming up soon, and he'd agonized on what to get Abby. After talking to his Mom, he decided to get her something from Amazon and quit worrying about it. He picked out a beautiful neckless and got back to his exercising within minutes after picking the gift.

Mr. Booker's friend, the agent Dale Williams, had come to Billy's home one day after school and talked to him and his parents. Mr. Williams explained a great deal to the family about Billy's future. He seemed to think Billy had a great chance of being drafted in the first few rounds if he had a good season next year.

"Mr. and Mrs. Tankersly, I would love to be Billy's agent, as I think he has a future, but to be honest, you should not hire an agent until after Billy gets drafted. If a player already has an agent, major league teams will not draft you as high, Billy, because they know they will have to pay the agent and you. Well, they pay you, but with an agent, they know you are going to be paying someone, so that holds them back", said Mr. Williams.

"So, do you think I will be drafted for sure after I graduate, Mr. Williams?" asked Billy.

"Billy, I think your chances are strong," replied the agent. He added, "Of course, even if you have a fantastic year, the chance of you being drafted high are probably lessened because of your age."

Mr. Williams left, shaking Mr. Tankersly's hand and giving his Mom a hug.

"Well, Billy, it sounds like you've got your work cut out for you," said his Dad. "In fact, you don't have to mow yards next year." That was the best news Billy could hear at that moment.

Christmas was a fun celebration at the Tankersly home with Abigale, Cameron, and Monica all joining them. Billy's gift to Abigale was perfect, and he was glad his Mom had advised him. He had not been spending as much time with Abby, explaining that he was exercising each day in his basement to get stronger. They all wanted to see Billy's exercise equipment, so after dinner and opening gifts, they headed to the basement.

"Wow, Billy, you've got more equipment than I do," said Cameron, trying out one piece after another. Billy's parents had purchased a new piece each year for the last three years, as Christmas presents. This year, his folks gave him a "Power Bag" that was supposed to strengthen a player's wrists and forearms. He read all about it as Cameron, and the girls helped him unpack and set it up.

"Hey, listen to this," Billy told the group. "Lance Berkman, who used to play for the Astro's used this, and he was powerful," said Billy. "He hit 366 home runs", Billy read, "which is five more than Joe DiMaggio."

After getting it set up, they all tried to use it, including the girls. Billy could see immediately that this would strengthen his wrists and forearms. He was ready for everyone to leave so he could spend time on it. He knew he'd be more powerful next year.

32

Graduating Early

Billy turned 15 in January, but there was no practice, other than in his basement. The roads were too covered with snow for anyone to get anywhere. Billy had received another new pair of spikes for his birthday, and they had Esky's name on them. All Billy could think about was how much better he was going to be.

He'd used the Power Bag for nearly two weeks, and there was no doubt, his forearms were getting stronger. He got on the scales in his basement one night and realized he'd gained another 10 pounds and was now 6' 1 ½".

In late February, the Yankees had their first practice. In batting practice, he tried to hit the ball hard every time up. One thing he'd watched on YouTube was how the good players always waited for their pitch and hit with their wrists late in the pitch. He listened to several major leaguers say in videos, "This is not easy when you are facing a pitcher who can hit 100 mph on the radar gun and then throw a changeup that slows to 70 mph."

"Coach," Billy asked. "How fast do the pitchers in the tournaments throw?"

"Billy, we will see a few guys this year that will hit 93-94 on their fastball", Coach Heier told him.

"Do we have anyone that can throw that fast?" Billy asked.

"Not on any of our teams, but next week, Carlos Garcia from the Royals is coming out to show all of us what it's like to face major league pitching," the coach said, raising his eyebrows like this was an important secret that he'd finally told the boys.

Billy could hardly wait until practice next week. He was the first in the cage to face Carlos. The first pitch came in so fast that Billy didn't even get the bat off his shoulders. He said out loud, "Just waiting for my pitch."

Carlos laughed and said, "Do you want me to slow it down because that one was right over the heart of the plate?"

Billy felt pretty sheepish, but he yelled back at Carlos, "No, throw me your best heat."

The ball jumped off his bat like none before. He hit it over the right fielder's head, and it rolled to the next practice diamond.

"Billy, you just hit the best fastball I've thrown in two years," yelled Carlos at Billy. Coach Heier had a radar gun and yelled, "That was 99 mph, Carlos."

"If you can hit like that on a regular basis, Billy, you are going to get drafted high after you graduate," said Carlos in front of all the other players.

When he got home and told his Dad, Mr. Tankersly had something he wanted to talk over with Billy.

"Billy, you know how you wanted to graduate early so you could get drafted?" his Dad asked.

"Sure," Billy said, wondering where his Dad was going with this conversation.

"Well, son, we know that you have been taking extra classes all year," began Billy's Dad. "To be honest, you have shown your Mom and me that you are very dedicated as you've kept your grades up. Also, we believe you have improved your baseball skills enough that you do have a chance to get drafted once you are out of high school. We have an idea we would like to run by you", began his Dad.

"Since you already have extra credits for two semesters, would you like to enroll in enough classes next year to graduate by December?" his Dad asked.

"What is this all about?" Billy wondered.

"Here is our thinking, Billy," continued his Dad. "The major league draft is held every June. If you graduate early, you will be able to devote the entire second semester to baseball. You will be able to use the Academy, as well as continue to strengthen your body in the basement. Maybe Mr. Booker will even run with you more, and if anyone can help you, it's Mr. Booker, as you well know."

"Dad and Mom, are you serious?" Billy's mind was racing a mile a minute.

"Yes, Billy," he heard his Dad say. "We have talked to Coach Heier, Mr. Elton and Mr. Booker about this. All of them agree that there is a good chance for you to get drafted next June if you have a good year."

Billy was stunned. Even though he'd enrolled in extra classes this semester, he never dreamed his parents would be encouraging him to graduate early.

"I'll do it," he said, hugging each of them. He was now taller and weighed more than his Dad, and had to stoop to hug his Mom.

As soon as he left the living room, he was Skyping Bobby, who he hadn't talked to for the longest time since Bobby had moved to Austin.

"Hey Bobby, guess what?" said Billy.

"There you go again. You always do this to me, Billy", laughed Bobby. "How many guesses do I get?"

"Three," teased Billy.

"OK, you have a new girlfriend," guessed Bobby, only to find out that wasn't it.

"You are moving to Austin?" Bobby guessed, again wrong.

"Billy, I have no idea, what?" Bobby said, with a little impatience in his voice.

"I am going to enroll in enough classes to be able to graduate next December," explained Billy.

"Why would you want to do that?" asked his life-long friend.

"Well, it's sort of a long story. On the trip to Phoenix, I had some major league scouts talk to me, and then when I got home, I spoke to a real live agent", Billy told Bobby, watching his eyes get bigger and bigger, as Billy was explaining.

"I'm pretty sure I can be drafted next year, Bobby," Billy said.

"Are you kidding me, like usual, Billy?" Bobby asked.

"No, this is serious Bobby," answered Billy. "Obviously, I need to have a great year this year, but if I do, some people who have been talking to Dad and Mom seem to think I definitely will be drafted. No one knows how high, but that will be determined how I play this year."

"Wow Billy," shouted Bobby, putting his hands on the top of his head, leaning back in his chair trying to take it all in. "That is phenomenal."

"Now, I guess I have to have the best year of my career," laughed Billy.

The two boys talked for about 30 minutes, and Billy found out that Bobby was 5'11 now and weighed around 180. They both laughed at how big the other was, remembering the scrawny kids they were when they started playing ball.

"It seems like playing on the Rockets that first year was a lifetime ago, Billy," Bobby mused.

33

Injury

The Yankee's first tournament was in Kansas City, much to his folk's delight. They were playing the KC Terminals at the 3 & 2 Stadium. Before the game, the coach gathered the team together at the third base dugout.

"Guys, we had a great season last year," started the coach. "We'd almost have to go undefeated this year to match it, but what do you say.....you want to go undefeated?" asked the coach with a big smile.

The team all yelled, "Yes" at the same time. It was so good to be playing baseball again.

The Yankees were the visitors. Billy was a little surprised that he was not leading off, but batting third, just like he did for the Rockets. Carter Colbert was a new kid on the team this year, and the coach decided to bat him leadoff, enabling Billy's ever developing power to be more utilized than if he was leading off.

"Way to go, Carter," the team chanted as Carter started the game with a single. Cameron was batting second, and he hit a line drive over the shortstop's head for another single. Carter held at second.

After taking a couple of practice swings, Billy stepped into the batter's box, only to hear the catcher saying, "Have you ever hit a curve?" Billy didn't turn around, but said, "No, that's my weakness," hoping the catcher would give the pitcher the sign for a curve. Sure enough, the first pitch was a slow breaking curve, and Billy hit the stuffing out of the ball for a three-run home run. As he crossed home plate, the team came out to greet him. It felt great to get a home run his first at-bat this season. He hoped there were scouts in the stands.

The Yankees won the first series and then their second series played in Prairie Village, Kansas. Billy was off to a good start with three home runs, and five stolen bases in his first two series. But, it was his defense that his Dad raved about after the last series was over.

"Billy, your defense has really improved," stated his Dad, who was riding in the passenger seat because Billy was driving.

"Dad, I've really been working on my footwork in the basement," Billy told his Dad.

"It shows, Billy," complimented his Dad, smiling proudly.

Billy spent more and more time running and taking hitting practice at the Academy. He could see that he was getting faster and stronger. Mr. Booker would run with him a couple of times a week, always with more advice. He felt he had two coaches. Mr. Booker and Coach Heier.

"I guess, counting Dad, I've got three coaches," Billy thought.

The next tournament was in Emporia, Kansas. Billy recalled driving through Emporia on the way to Austin. The game was played on the college field. Billy had a good first game. He homered, drove in three runs and stole two bases. The Yankees were off to another great season.

In the second game, Billy came up with no one on and hit a sharp line drive to right. He saw the first base coach waving his hands for him to go to second, but as he rounded the bag, he felt something snap. He limped into second base, and they tagged him out. The coach came running out to second base to see what had happened, as Billy was now laying on the ground, moaning.

"What happened, Billy?" the coach asked frantically.

"I don't know," Billy cried out.

"Can you stand, Billy?" the coach asked.

"No coach. It hurts too badly", Billy screamed.

Jim Tankersly stood up in the stands with his wife, hoping their son was OK, but he could tell, he wasn't. The coach and the assistant coach carried Billy off the field.

Jim was standing behind the dugout, asking if they needed to take Billy to the hospital. Billy heard the coach say, "I think you should."

Billy had never been on a longer ride. He was in pain and just wanted someone to take the pain away. He had never experienced anything like this. Once they reached the hospital, it seemed like hours before they got a doctor to see him. Finally, a doctor came out, asked Billy to do a couple of things with his leg, that Billy couldn't do. He was told they were going to have to admit him to the hospital for x-rays and other tests.

"What is it?" Billy asked the doctor.

"Son, I think you've either torn or sprained your knee. "It might be an ACL injury," the doctor answered. "But, let's see what the x-ray and MRI say," added the doctor.

Billy was scared. He looked too big to be crying, but he feared his major league dreams might be over, and he was unable to hold back the tears. His knee hurt badly. The nursing staff wheeled him on a gurney to room number 323 and gave him some medicine for the pain. By now, the rest of the team was at the hospital. Billy didn't want them to see his tears. All his dreams were hinging on the tests. The results would not be back until the morning. His Dad and Mom stayed with him, trying to encourage him that maybe it was just a bad sprain. For maybe the first time in his life, Billy prayed.

He didn't sleep at all, or if he did, it didn't seem like it. Finally, the doctor walked into the room.

"Your son has a grade 1 or 2 sprain", said the doctor to Billy's parents. "He will need to stay in the hospital another night, to let us do further tests," said the doctor without emotion.

"How long will the recovery take?" asked Mr. Tankersly.

"It could take three weeks to six months," the doctor replied, indicating therapy to strengthen the knee could help shorten the time, but he really did not want to say until they had done further tests.

"Six months?" Billy cried out.

"Yes son, it could take that long," the doctor didn't do anything to make Billy feel better.

After the doctor had left, Billy asked his parents, "Do you ever pray for something?"

"Yes son, we pray for you every night," his Dad replied.

"You never go to church," Billy commented.

"No Billy, we don't, but we read the Bible and pray together every night," Mr. Tankersly said.

"Why haven't you ever told me anything about the Bible or praying?" Billy asked.

"Billy, we felt that was a decision for you to make. We knew that, someday, God would come into your life because of our prayers", his Dad explained.

"I think I've found him because that's all I did during the night," cried Billy. "I thanked God that he would heal me because baseball is the only thing I've ever wanted to do. I told God I couldn't see my life without baseball in it. If he would heal me that I would do my best to help other kids reach their goals."

"Good prayer, Billy," praised his Dad. "My guess is that God will answer your prayer," Mr. Tankersly told his son.

The day passed slowly with more and more tests. Billy was scared. Night came, and he wasn't in as much pain, probably because of the medicine they were giving him, but he seemed to be more at peace.

"Dad and Mom, after praying, I felt God was going to answer my prayer, and I believe it's not going to be something as serious as the doctor said this morning," whispered Billy as he finally fell to sleep.

The next morning, bright and early, the doctor came in. Billy couldn't tell if he had good or bad news, but he still felt peaceful. The doctor lifted Billy's leg, twisted it as much as it would twist, and informed the family that Billy's sprain was not as bad as they initially thought. Billy could go home that day, start exercising his leg, and he would be "good to go" in seven to 10 days, mainly because of being in such good shape.

As they left the hospital, Billy sat in the back with his leg propped up all the way back to Kansas City.

He was already flexing the muscles in his leg, thinking, "Thank you, God."

"Dad and Mom, did you hear if the Yankees won that game and the last one?" he asked.

"They did, Billy, but just barely," answered his Dad. "They won the game after you got hurt, 5-4 and the last game on Sunday, they beat the Hutchinson Pirates, 6-4".

34

Understands Bonus

Billy was able to go to the Yankees games the following weekend, but could not play. He sat on the bench, yelling encouragement to each batter. They won all three games and were still undefeated.

The following weekend, the Yankees played in Sedalia, Missouri, and met a team that was also undefeated, the Springfield Soro's. Billy finally got to play. He had three hits, two stolen bases, and one home run as the Yankees won the first game 10-3. His knee had felt a little stiff but loosened fast and didn't bother him again.

The second game started with Billy hitting a two-run home run in the first inning, giving the Yankees a 2-0 lead. The A's, another good team, fought back but were not able to catch the Yankees. The final score was 9-3, and Billy had two more hits, line drive singles, and he stole three bases. There was one more game Sunday.

The Tankersly's reserved a hotel room in Springfield and Billy's Dad congratulated him for a good game but didn't say a whole lot more. Finally, Billy broke the silence about the game.

"Dad, did you know there were scouts there today?" Billy asked.

Billy's Dad had pondered if he should tell his son what he learned at the game. He decided to tell Billy about what happened at the games.

"Billy, one of the scouts, came up to me, and asked me if you were going to graduate at 16", spoke Mr.

Tankersly. "I told them I thought you were, and he said that the way you played ball, you had a chance to be drafted," added Billy's Dad.

"Truthfully, Dad?" Billy inquired. He believed his Dad but wanted to hear more.

"They showed me a potential draft list that had been put together by some sportswriter. Your name was on the list", his Dad told Billy. "But you were closer to the bottom than the top."

That made Billy even more determined to work harder, and to play the best baseball he could. The Sunday game was another victory for the Yankees. They won, 7-4. Billy got a double, and two singles. He was happy that he had the singles because that gave him the chance to steal and steal he did. Four stolen bases. It was a good game.

After two more weekends of tournaments, the Yankees had won six more games. A man, who Billy did not know, approached him after the last game.

"Hey Billy, I'm RJ Kingman with the Astro's. We saw your name on a potential draft list and decided to watch you play. Of course, this is only a sports reporter putting together a list. It really has no bearing on anything but is a guide that got me to your game. Your folks tell me you are graduating in December, making you eligible for the June Draft", said Mr. Kingman

"So, do you think I'll really be drafted next year since I am finishing high school in December?" Billy, throwing all caution to the wind, asked the scout, Mr. Kingman.

"I think it depends on how you finish this year. Right now, from what your coach tells me, you are hitting .565, with 21 stolen bases already, and you were out for two weeks", Mr. Kingman told Billy. "Keep that up, and yes, you should be on some draft lists, but that doesn't mean you'll actually get drafted high. Major league teams used to think that a kid had to graduate from college to have the best chance, but in the last 10 years, high school draftees have fared better than college kids. However, only one player has been drafted in the first round before he's 17, Billy, because very few kids graduate at 16. That makes your chances of being drafted high, less than if you'd stayed in school another year", said Mr. Kingman.

Billy was stunned. He thought that would help him, and now he's hearing that taking all those extra classes may have been for naught.

Mr. Kingman continued. "You just never know, Billy, but some team could draft you in the early rounds, thinking you just might make the majors in 4-5 years. The problem with putting you high on a draft list is that only 4% of the kids we sign, make the majors", explained Mr. Kingman, "and you are very young."

Billy had been told by one scout earlier that he might want to go to Junior College for a year, because of those players, unlike players in a traditional four-year college, could be drafted at any time.

"Do you think I should go to junior college first, Mr. Kingman?" Billy asked.

"It's something for you to think about, Billy, but you can make that decision after the June draft. If you get drafted high, you might want to go ahead and sign, but if you get drafted in the later rounds, maybe junior college would be the best route", said Mr. Kingman.

"Keep in mind, Billy, there is a lot of money being offered by major league teams for first and second round picks," said Mr. Kingman. This is an investment for major league teams, and they are very selective with their picks. I have no idea where you will be drafted, but you might consider enrolling in a junior college if you are not drafted high. With one year of junior college experience behind you, it might move you up in the following year's draft", added the Astro's scout. Most first and second round picks will be signed for over $1,000,000 while those selected later might only get a little over $150,000.

The number staggered Billy. For some reason, he'd never looked at how much draft picks made. He knew that players like Alex Gordon would make more than $12,000,000 a year, but he'd never googled what a draft pick might make. He had just wanted to play ball.

Mr. Kingman departed wishing Billy good luck the rest of the year.

Carter had been standing off on the side, along with Cameron.

"Billy, what was that all about?" asked Cameron.

"I'm not sure what to make of it, guys. It was a scout for the Astro's, and he told me that I had a chance of being drafted next year, but maybe not very high, since I'm graduating in December", Billy told them.

"You are graduating in December, Billy?" Cameron asked.

Billy shook his head yes, still thinking about what Mr. Kingman told him.

"Are you serious, Billy?" Carter shot back. "Are you graduating early, so you can be in the draft?" asked Carter.

"Yes, Carter," answered Billy," but Mr. Kingman told me that only one player had been drafted in the first round under 17 so I may have made a mistake by taking all those extra classes to graduate in December", moaned Billy.

Cameron spoke first. "No matter what, Billy, that is fantastic." Carter joined in with his praise as the boys left the field.

35

Scouts Watching

The rest of the season went by fast. They Yankees were still undefeated, and Billy was noticing more people in the stands, who looked like they might be scouts, but no one talked to him. With two tournaments to go, including the championship tournament, Billy was still hitting over .500 and had 52 stolen bases. He loved his metal spikes and wanted to steal every time he got on, but sometimes, Coach Heier didn't give him the steal sign. Billy couldn't figure out why because he'd only been caught one time, but he figured Coach Heier knew what he was doing.

The first tournament turned out like all the rest. All Yankee wins. Billy stayed red hot in the batter box and in stealing bases. In this tournament, Billy had 9 hits, two home runs, one double and five stolen bases. He felt more and more confident that he would get drafted, but the question remained, "How high?"

His total passion for the game meant sacrificing many things, like going fishing with his Dad or playing tag football with the kids in the neighborhood. He realized he'd missed out on what most young boys do. But his heart was set on being a major leaguer and setting the stolen base record. Instead of doing what other kids did, he spent all his time exercising, running, and getting as much advice from Coach Heier and Mr. Booker as he could. He knew he was missing out on a lot of fun things his friends were doing. Still, he didn't regret it.

"I am going to get some major league team to draft me in one of the first rounds," he thought positively to himself.

The final tournament was in Wichita, and if the Yankees won the first two, there was a good chance they would be playing the Shockers in the final game. Mr. Booker had joined Billy and his Mom and Dad on the trip. His running coach talked baseball with him all the way to Wichita. They stayed in a Hyatt Place hotel, not far from the stadium.

After dinner, Mr. Booker and Billy sat outside by the pool.

"You've been around baseball so long now, Mr. Booker, what do you think my chances are of being drafted in the first or second round?" Billy asked.

"Billy, you are really a good player. You have so much potential, I think one day you will probably play in the majors", said Mr. Booker.

"But you didn't answer my question," Billy followed up.

"That is because I just don't know, Billy," Mr. Booker said. "Your age could work against you, but some team might find your young age attractive and take a chance when they draft. The major league teams sign players from other countries when they are 16 and give them healthy bonuses, so maybe one of the teams will look at you the same way."

"You talk to scouts, Mr. Booker", started Billy. "Have you heard anything from them about me?"

Mr. Booker looked at Billy and told him he had no more information. Billy was disappointed, but decided "No news is good news." He didn't know where he'd heard that, but as he laid down to go to sleep, he was more optimistic than a few hours ago and determined to have the best series he'd ever had.

The next morning, bright and early, the Tankersly's and Mr. Booker left for the first tournament game.

Coach Heier told the boys before the series that this was for all the marbles. If they could sweep the teams in the tournament, they could be the first team in the traveling league to finish undefeated. But this was a tournament for the best teams in the Midwest.

"We will be playing the Gove Indians the first game, and they've only lost four games all season," said the coach. They have a pitcher that not many teams can hit, so we've got to be smart when we are up at the plate. He's known to throw a lot of curves, but they seldom are over the plate, even though guys swing because the pitch looks good before the bottom drops out. So today, wait for your pitch, and you will get it", concluded the coach.

"Play Ball," yelled the ump. The Yankees were the home team. Billy liked being the "visiting" team better because the Yankees were ahead almost every game coming into the 7th inning. Since the Yankees usually had the lead, they didn't have to bat in the bottom of the inning. Billy figured it up one day and guessed that he lost 30 "at-bats" when his team was the home team, which in his mind, meant he could have added to his stolen base mark.

The game against the Gove Indians was the same as many others the Yankees had played this year. The game was over by the third inning because the Yankees led 9-1. Billy had homered and doubled by the third inning and stolen a base. By the time he got his third "at bat," he was ready to get a single, so he could steal second base and maybe third. He wanted the scouts to see how fast he was and did what he hoped. He singled, stole second and third and scored on Bill's double to left field. The game was over, just as fast as it started, Billy thought. They won with a lopsided score of 14-5.

After the game, the coach told them they would be playing the Topeka Twins in the afternoon game, who had also lost only four times all year.

"Coach, what is their pitcher like?" Billy asked.

"He throws a fastball that averages 93 miles per hour. He relies on that pitch. Because he throws so hard, he's a little wild. The same thing goes for him. Wait for your pitch", the Coach told the boys.

The game started with Carter leading off with a single.

"Way to go," screamed the guys on the bench. Coach told the team that since this was their last series, he wanted to see everyone showing high energy, chattering from the bench, and they were doing it.

Cameron singled, and up came up Billy, with the other team knowing he was the best hitter, and that he led the league in stolen bases.

"You think you can hit a 95 mph fastball, batter?" razzed the catcher as Billy stepped in.

"I'm going to hit it out of the park on the first pitch," said Billy back to the big catcher.

He had studied the pitcher during Carter and Cameron's at-bats and knew that he threw a flat fastball. It had no movement inside or out.

Billy swung at the first pitch. Before he left the batter's box, he knew it was a home run. As he started to run to first, laying his bat down slowly, as he left the batter box, he was pretty sure the catcher could hear him say, "Yeah, I can hit a fastball."

The Twins were a good ball club and came back to take the lead in the 4th, 4-3. Billy was up first, determined to hit another homer to tie the game. Coach Heier motioned for Billy to walk to third to talk to him.

"Billy, I want you to lay down a drag bunt. We need runners on base", said the coach.

Without hesitating, Billy said, "I'll get on."

In came the fastball, which was about all this pitcher could throw. Billy started running to first throwing his bat at the ball. It was still in his hands, but he felt like he was throwing it, and sure enough, he laid down a perfect drag bunt that no one was really expecting, and there wasn't even a throw to first. The coach did not give him the steal sign as Will was coming up to the plate. He had almost as much power as Billy. On the second pitch, he drilled one that sailed over the left fielder's outstretched glove and over the fence. The Yankees led again, 5-4. The game ended that way, and the Yankees had only one more game to win to go undefeated. But, they were playing the Wichita Shockers who had clobbered them in their first game a year ago. The Coach told them to get a good night's sleep because the team's undefeated season was almost a reality... just one more win.

"Billy, why did you drag bunt in the 6th inning?" his Dad asked on the way to the hotel.

"Because Coach Heier told me to, Dad," Billy answered a little sarcastically. Surely his Dad knew he wanted to hit a home run to tie the game.

"Billy, you could have answered that with a better tone in your voice," said his Dad, firmly.

"I'm sorry Dad. I wanted to hit a home run, but when the coach told me to drag bunt, what choice did I have?" Billy answered with a much better attitude.

"None. I just wondered, Billy, because you knew the scouts were there and if that was your decision to show off your speed, and versatility, or the coach's decision", explained Mr. Tankersly.

"Dad, I wanted to swing for the fence," laughed Billy.

"Did any of the scouts talk to you today, Dad?" Billy wanted to know.

"Yes Billy, one scout told me he thought you would be drafted, but he had no idea what round" he replied.

His Dad explained to him that scouts would not know. Draft picks were the decision of the General Manager's and Major League coaches.

36

Scouts Impressed

Sunday's game against the Shockers drew a huge crowd. Traveling baseball wasn't mentioned much in the Kansas City papers, but in Wichita, it was big news. The traveling baseball team was even named after the college team in Wichita.

"The Yankees versus the Shockers, the best two travel baseball teams in the Midwest, with potential major leaguers on both rosters," he read in the Wichita newspaper that morning. Billy wondered if they were referring to him, but no matter, the article had drawn a big crowd in the grandstands. Before the game, Billy looked over the crowd to see if he could find any scouts he recognized but was drawn back to reality with Coach Heier calling the team together.

"Guys, you know how big today's game is," started the coach. "Billy Mustang is pitching for the Shockers, and he has not lost all year. He is probably a first round pick in the draft next year, but I know you can hit him", continued the coach.

"What does he throw?" Cameron asked.

"Everything," answered the Coach. "His fastball reaches 97 mph while his curve will come in around 70 mph, so like all year, you have to be patient to hit your pitch, not what he wants you to swing at."

A small portion of the crowd cheered as the Yankees took the field. The home team had been determined with a flip of the coin by the umpires before the game. The Yankees won the toss, but this was obviously a home game for the Shockers.

Sam Meddelton, the starting pitcher for the Yankees, had not allowed a run in his last two games but had given up four runs in one inning about mid-season. Billy and the rest of the team just hoped he would pitch like he had the past two weeks.

"Strike one," yelled the ump. Sam's first pitch was a fastball on the inside of the plate. Billy knew the hitter was probably a kid who would be drafted, and he hoped Sam could get him out.

On the next pitch, a ground ball was hit to Billy's left. He scooped the ball up behind second, twirled around and threw a perfect strike to first. A few people in the grandstands cheered. After a fly ball to Carter and a grounder to Will, the Yankees came up to bat in the bottom of the first.

"Cameron, I read the paper this morning, and this Mustang guy only has one weakness," Billy began telling his good friend. "He gets nervous at the start of big games, so now is the time to get to him," encouraged Billy.

"OK, most big games," thought Billy as Carter and Cameron both struck out.

"You can hit him, Billy," yelled the players from the dugout as Billy settled in the batter's box.

Three straight pitches that must have hit the black part of the plate because Billy didn't think any of them were strikes, but he was called out. Seldom did Billy strike out. This was the first time he struck out where he didn't even lift the bat off his shoulder. He turned to the umpire, stared at him for a good two seconds before saying, "Where exactly was that pitch?"

The umpire remained calm and told Billy it was on the inside corner. Billy shook his head "No," but walked to the dugout, got his glove and ran to his position. Like the first inning, the leadoff batter hit a sharp grounder to Billy's left. Again, he made a spectacular play, beating the runner to first by half a step.

"Maybe they realize I'm a future major leaguer," thought Billy as his teammates threw the ball around the infield.

It was the 4th inning before Billy got to bat again. The score was still 0-0 with the Yankees not even getting a hit so far. He was determined to change that.

"Strike one," yelled the ump, on a pitch Billy knew was outside. He stepped out of the box, not looking at the ump, but making his displeasure known to everyone in the stadium, including the ump, with the expression on his face.

On the next pitch, Billy let it go by because it was high.

"Strike two," yelled the umpire again. This time, Billy stepped out of the box, turned toward the ump and started to say something when he heard Mr. Booker up in the stands yelling, "Next pitch, Billy." He turned back toward the pitcher without saying a word.

He was confident that the Shocker pitcher would throw him another fastball since Billy hadn't taken the bat off his shoulder. He was ready.

He swung nice and easy and hit a line drive over second base. As he rounded first, he was happy to have finally gotten a pitch he could hit. As he looked over to third, he knew he'd get the steal sign.

After the Shocker pitcher had tried to pick him off, unsuccessfully, Billy took off on the first pitch. The catcher's throw sailed into centerfield, and Billy didn't stop at second. He had beaten the wild throw by so much, he was able to get to third standing up. Will hit a short fly ball to right field. Billy tagged, hoping to beat the throw. It was a bang, bang play at the plate, but Billy knew he was safe. He looked up at the ump who had his arms spread out, indicating he was safe before yelling, "Safe." The Yankees led 1-0.

In the 6th inning, the Shockers scored three runs to take a 3-1 lead going into the bottom of the sixth. The Yankees were retired in order. Their undefeated season was on the line.

Coach Heier called the team together before they took the field in the top of the 7th.

"OK guys, we've come this far without losing. Let's get them out, and come back to win the game in the bottom of the 7th", Coach Heier challenged his team.

The Shockers didn't score, so the game and undefeated season were coming down to the last inning. Billy was going to bat 4th, and he was praying that Josh, Carter, and Cameron would get on base, somehow, someway, so he could win the game.

Josh hit a grounder toward the Shocker's shortstop. He picked it up smoothly and then threw it in the dirt so low the first baseman could not scoop up. Billy yelled to Carter, "This is our chance. Get a hit."

But after four straight balls, Carter walked. Billy thought, "Maybe the umpire is feeling guilty about all the bad calls he made at the first of the game."

"Let's go, Cameron," yelled Billy as the stands were coming alive with people cheering for the Yankees, which surprised Billy.

Billy Mustang, the Shocker's starter who had allowed only two hits, looked nervous. Billy yelled, "he's nervous, Cam." He was glad he'd read the paper that morning. The newspaper said "At the start of big games," but Billy was seeing him nervous here in the 7th. After two straight outside pitches to Cameron, the Shocker coach walked out to the mound to talk to his pitcher.

It didn't do any good. Cameron walked on four pitches, just like Carter. The bases were loaded for Billy. He knew he could hit Mustang as he already had one hit against him. A single would tie the game.

The Shocker coach walked to the mound, waved his left hand in the air, signaling that he wanted a lefty to face the left-handed hitting Billy Tankersly.

Billy watched the new pitcher, a kid who was introduced over the PA system as Butch Kelly. Billy didn't know anything about him but watched his warmups like a hawk. All he threw in the warmups were curves, and Billy's mind drifted back to the days when his Dad was throwing him nothing but curves. He knew he could hit this guy.

"Play ball," yelled the ump after Kelly had taken his warmups. Billy stepped into the batter's box full of confidence. He knew he was going to get a curve.

"Strike one," yelled the ump as a 93 mph fastball sped over the heart of the plate. Billy was so convinced that he'd see a curve that once again, his bat remained on his shoulder. He stepped out, got his focus back and watched two straight pitches way outside, both fastballs.

With the count 2-1, and the bases loaded, Billy guessed fastball, only to see a curve break over the heart of the plate, with Billy not budging. He knew it was a strike, even before hearing the ump yell it out. The count was now, 2-2 and Billy had no idea what type of pitch he would see.

It was a fastball that nearly hit Billy as he fell to the ground. "Ball three," Billy heard the umpire say as he got up, dusting himself off. The count was now 3 & 2 with the bases loaded. Billy thought to himself, "He threw nothing but curves in his warmups, he almost hit me with a fastball. I think he's more comfortable with his curve and he's going to throw me a curve ball."

Kelly went into his windup. Billy watched the ball come out of his hand. He saw spin. The same kind of spin that Billy had seen from his Dad. He knew it was a curve.

The ball left his bat far faster than it had been pitched. It kept climbing, and before Billy was to first base, the first base umpire was twirling his hand around in a circle, indicating that Billy had just hit a grand slam home run to win the championship game.

The team rushed the plate and nearly kept Billy from touching it. As soon as he did, the team lifted him above their heads, carrying him back to the dugout shouting, "Billy, Billy, Billy."

Billy Tankersly felt good about his future.

37

Focus

Now it was time for Billy to really get to work, developing his skills, before the draft. He hadn't decided if he would play at all next season, or just continue his workouts, improving his bat speed, his foot speed, and overall defense waiting for the draft. Of course, Billy still had one semester of school to finish. He decided he was not going to waste a day.

Upon returning from the Wichita tournament, he called Bobby, and saw Abigale, telling them both that he was getting focused on what he needed to do, even though he had no idea if he'd be drafted.

Billy studied everything he could find about baseball. He saw what sportswriters were predicting for the June draft, including a listing of the top 50 amateur players. He was not included.

Mr. Booker gave him a glimmer of hope one day while they were running.

"Billy, I had a man call me, asking about you," said Mr. Booker as they ran together again. "He was from the Royals. They will be drafting last in the first round", continued the Hall of Fame Groundskeeper.

"What did he ask?" Billy inquired.

"The usual things, how fast you are, what I saw as your weaknesses, strengths, etc.", answered Mr. Booker.

"So what did you tell him my weakness are?" Billy wanted to know.

"Your age," was the answer Billy didn't want to hear.

"That's my biggest weakness, Mr. Booker?" Billy asked.

Mr. Booker stopped running and got a serious look on his face.

"Billy, do you remember me telling you that graduating early might not be the best for you?" Mr. Booker reminded him of a conversation at the start of the season.

"Yes sir, I remember, but it was something I had to do on my own," said Billy.

"That is the weakness, Billy. You are stubborn. You don't always listen to sound advice being given to you by people older and more experienced than you", replied Mr. Booker. "Sometimes, it appears you think you know it all."

"Really, Mr. Booker?" Billy asked as this was not something he'd even considered. "You mean I don't know everything?" Billy laughed.

"See, right there, you are making light about what I just said was your biggest weakness," spoke Mr. Booker in a scolding manner. "How do you expect to improve in the minors with coaches giving you advice if you don't take it seriously?" he asked Billy.

They'd started running again and were at Billy's house, but Mr. Booker continued.

"Billy, as I told the man from the Royals, you have all the tools. You can hit for average, for power, have speed not many others have had, and an arm that is among the best. To top that off, you are extremely athletic, as witnessed by those two defensive plays you had against the Shockers", added Mr. Booker. "But, you lack maturity," he concluded.

Billy asked the man, "How do I get maturity?"

Mr. Booker paused, smiled, and gave him a simple answer that Billy did not like. "You add a year or two to your age."

As Billy thanked Mr. Booker for being honest with him, he went inside to find his parents in an argument. He didn't know what it was about, but heard his Dad say, "Let's pray about it."

Billy still didn't understand this "praying" bit, but he did notice that the argument stopped right after they'd prayed. That night when getting into bed, Billy prayed for God to give him maturity. But, the first thing he heard when he woke up was, "Billy, take the trash out."

"I'm not even awake yet. I'll do it later", quipped Billy, realizing immediately that apparently his prayer had not been answered overnight. After getting up, and heading to the basement to work out, he realized he needed to do it now.

"OK, I'll do it right now, and get it over with, Mom," Billy yelled.

Once he had the trash emptied, he told his Dad and Mom what Mr. Booker said to him yesterday.

"He told a man from the Royals that my biggest weakness was my age because I lacked maturity," Billy explained.

Billy's Dad laughed, which caused his Mom to laugh. He got the picture. They agreed with Mr. Booker.

"OK, what do I have to do to get maturity?" he asked, knowing it was the same question he'd asked Mr. Booker.

"Billy, you are going on 16. There are very few kids your age that have maturity because it comes from experience in life, from learning from mistakes", his

Mom told him. Billy was not used to his Mom being the one to answer his baseball-related questions, and then he realized that maybe this wasn't just a baseball question.

The conversation ended, and Billy charged off to the basement again to start working on the Power Bag, but his mind was on what his Mom said. For the first time since he'd enrolled in extra classes to be able to graduate early, he thought, "maybe I really did make the wrong decision."

38

Major Decision

School started, and Billy was taking the extra classes that cut down on his time for practice. He continued questioning his own decision. His confidence level dropped, and he decided it was time to talk to Coach Heier. Instead of running with Mr. Booker that day, Billy headed straight to the Academy to see if his Coach was there. He was.

"Coach, a week or so ago, Mr. Booker told me a man from the Royals had contacted him and asked what my biggest weakness was, and he answered that it was my age", Billy told his coach.

"Billy, I've also been contacted by baseball people about you, asking me the same question," the Coach said to him. "My answer was a little different than Mr. Booker's. I've told each of them that you have very few weaknesses and I have no doubt that you will one day being playing in the majors."

That brightened Billy's day and made him start thinking about his strengths instead of his weakness. He found out by focusing on his strengths, they just got better, and the weaknesses seemed to disappear. He realized his bat speed had improved. One day after school, he had Mr. Booker time him to first, like he had started doing two years ago.

"Wow, Billy, you've knocked a tenth of a second off," Mr. Booker told him. "You are now running to first as fast as most major leaguers," shouted Mr. Booker. "Let's time you to third," the man instructed.

Billy took off from the plate, rounding each base in the way he'd been taught and as he slid into third, he knew it was the fastest he'd ever made it.

Mr. Booker yelled from the plate, "Billy that was your fastest time since we started clocking you."

Billy went home that night, more determined than ever to focus on his strengths, and determined to show everyone that he had the maturity to play professional baseball.

It was still warm outside when Thanksgiving arrived. Billy and Mr. Booker were running three days a week after school, but Billy knew the first snow would happen soon. When it first started to snow, around Christmas, Billy began working out at the Academy more. Coach Heier took him under his wing and gave him advice on how to play better defense, and how to recognize a pitch even better than what his Dad had taught him. He was listening intently to everything the Coach said to him.

Then came his graduation in December, and he had all the time in the world to improve. He worked out most days from dawn until late in the night doing hitting exercises, running, strengthening his legs, and upper body. He spent four to five hours at the Academy doing nothing but practicing his hitting. Many days, Coach Heier would pitch to him. Other days, one of the students would pitch to him. He had stopped growing physically earlier than most, and he was still 6'1 1/2". His weight had actually decreased because of the extensive workouts he put himself through. The almost 16-year-old was pushing himself to the limit every day.

In January, Billy had to make a decision to play on the team until he was drafted, or just continue working out.

"Coach, what do you think?" Billy asked Coach Heier.

"Well, Billy, have you seen the Baseball America potential amateur draft lists?" the Coach asked.

"No, sir. I quit looking at all that a couple of months ago, deciding that I needed to work on my strengths and not worry about what I could not change", Billy answered.

"That shows me some maturity, Billy. But to answer your question about playing this year, or continuing to work out, you are in fact listed on some of the potential draft lists", the coach told Billy.

"How high?" Billy wanted to know.

"Pretty high, Billy, on a couple of lists," the coach began. Billy had decided on his own that he would not play this year but continue working out until the draft.

"I think if baseball people were to see you play this spring, you could climb the list even higher," the coach told him. "Keep in mind, Mr. Booker was correct in the fact that your age is your biggest drawback right now. About the only way to overcome that is to let baseball people see you play this spring. If you do not play, they are only going to remember last year when you were 15", Coach Heier concluded.

Billy thought about what the coach said all the way home. As he entered, he told his folks that he thought he should play on the Yankees at least until the draft.

39

New Goal

Billy started practicing with the team two weeks later, and by now, he couldn't resist anymore. He searched the Internet for all the projected amateur draft lists. He found his name in all of them. His ranking ranged from late in the 5th round to high in the 3rd round. Comments associated with his name ranged from "worth a chance" to "too young." Then he read an article about the trend in the amateur draft was more and more toward young players.

The more he studied, the more he wanted to talk to an agent. He found out that most, if not all, players selected in the first two rounds had agents. He needed to remember to ask Mr. Booker why they had not gotten him an agent.

Billy was determined to get drafted as high as possible, and started to make his own projections. He figured since the Royals won the World Series last year, they would be drafting last in the first round. Could he improve enough in two months of playing tournaments, before the draft, that his favorite team would draft him?

During practice, Billy pulled Cameron aside one day.

"Cam, do you know you are on some of the projected draft lists?" Billy asked.

"Yeah, I follow them, but am projected below you in each of the projections," replied Cameron.

"It's sort of crazy how varied the projections are," added Billy. "I saw you as high as a third-round pick, but until reading the lists, I didn't realize you were a year older than me."

Cameron explained to Billy that he'd been held back a year at one point, but really didn't tell any of the baseball players.

"Why were you held back?" Billy asked.

"My parents went through a divorce, and I just didn't adjust very well being moved from one parent to the other," Cameron explained. "It was really hard, Billy, and I just quit doing about everything. Baseball was the only thing that meant anything to me", added Cameron.

"I'm really sorry you had to go through that, Cam. Maybe it made you a better baseball player because you worked harder at it", encouraged Billy.

"Let's hope we both get drafted, Billy," added Cam as he put on his catcher's mask to go catch batting practice.

Billy was hitting the ball all over the field. He was playing spectacular defense and was getting a lot of "great play, Billy" comments from the coaches and his teammates during the practices. He could hardly wait until their first tournament.

It was now February, and the Royals were just starting Spring Training. Billy remembered the feeling of being in Surprise, Arizona at the Royals camp and wished he could be there right now.

After getting home one night from practice, Billy read in Wikipedia that Baseball Prospectus writer Rany Jazayerli's latest study from 1965 to the present showed younger players were returning more value to major league teams that college graduates. He read that a player by the name of Alfredo Escalera had been drafted by the Royals at 17 years, 114 days in the 8th round. The youngest player drafted in the First-Year Player Drafts was a Benjamin Pelletier, who was only 16 years, 292 days old when the Phillies drafted him in the 34th round.

Billy figured that by the time he was drafted and then signed, he would be 16 years, and 183 days old. He made up his mind that night that he was going to set a new record for the youngest player ever drafted in the Amateur draft.

Billy had read some place that when you set a goal, you need to burn all bridges behind and tell others what you were going to do, so he decided to Skype Bobby to tell him.

"Hey, Bobby, what's up?" Billy asked.

"Well, we've played in two tournaments so far, and have won all our games," Bobby told Billy. "I saw you on several projected draft lists, Billy. "I sort of wish I'd finished school early like you did, but I'll be on the lists next year," Bobby dreamed out loud.

"Bobby, I'm not really sure I made the right decision," Billy started explaining to his best friend how he felt about it all. "So far, the youngest player ever drafted in the June draft was 16 years, 292 days old, but he wasn't drafted until the 34th round", Billy continued.

"You aren't even going to be 17 yet when the draft happens", said Bobby. "Are you willing to be drafted in a lower round?"

"I don't know, Bobby," said Billy, "but I have really improved over the winter by pushing myself on the exercise equipment, the batting cages, and running sprints daily trying to cut a 1/10 of a second off my time to first base. I have set a goal, Bobby and intend to be the youngest ever drafted", Billy finally blurted out.

"You are kidding me, Billy," said Bobby very seriously. "Do you really think you can be drafted before you are even 17?" Bobby asked.

Billy paused for a minute before answering, something he seldom did. "Bobby, you are the only one who knows what I'm about to tell you, not even my folks," started Billy. "I've set a goal. I am going to be drafted by the Royals in the first round", said Billy confidently.

"That's a mighty big goal," chirped Bobby, not knowing if his friend was kidding, and if not, thinking it was an unrealistic goal. "Are you kidding, Billy?" he asked. He started to tell Billy he needed to set a realistic goal, but before he could utter a word, Billy broke in.

"Between you and me, Bobby, that's my goal," said Billy. "I'm not even telling my folks, but am going to play with the Yankees until the June draft, hoping the scouts will see how much I've improved," concluded Billy.

The boys got off Skype, and Bobby wondered if Billy was setting himself up for a huge disappointment.

40

Workout for Royals

In March, the Yankees played in their first tournament. They won all three games in that tournament and in the next two as well. The games were going by quickly. Billy was playing baseball like he'd never played before. He was hitting home runs, stealing bases and making spectacular plays on defense.

He had been hitting cleanup for the first time in his life and made Coach Heier's decision look like that of a brilliant coach. Billy was driving in so many runs that the Yankees didn't have a close game until the fourth tournament. In that game, they came from behind to win in the last inning on a long home run off Billy's bat. That was his 5th home run in 9 games. He also had nine stolen bases, of which he was more proud than his home runs. Billy loved stealing a base. Nothing was more exciting to him.

In the fourth tournament of the year at the Sunday game, Mr. Booker asked Billy to meet him at the car after the game. He had no idea what Mr. Booker wanted to tell him, but he was glad he was there to see him play. He was determined to have a good game.

He ended up that Sunday having one of the best games he'd ever had. He hit two home runs and a single. Naturally, he stole second when he hit the single, but more importantly, he made three defensive plays that even Coach Heier couldn't believe.

After the game, which the Yankees won 9-2, he remembered Mr. Booker wanted to talk to him. He walked over to the car, carrying his lucky bat.

"Hi, Mr. Booker", announced Billy as he approached his friend and mentor. "What's up?" he asked.

"Billy, the Royals would like for you to come out to Surprise for a tryout," Mr. Booker told him. "Since you have been rising on the draft lists, the Royals would like to confirm that the numbers they have been receiving on you from the Stats service are painting an accurate picture. They are very impressed with what they've been hearing and reading", said Mr. Booker.

"Mr. Booker, I know you would not kid me about something like this", started Billy, with wide eyes. "Are you telling me that there is a chance the Royals might draft me?" asked Billy.

"I guess it all depends on how you do at the tryout, Billy," Mr. Booker answered. "Of course, only the Royals know who they want to draft and how high up," added Billy's running coach and mentor. "However, for them to ask me to have you come out for a tryout is very encouraging news, Billy," said Mr. Booker. "You will be receiving a formal invitation from their office tomorrow."

He explained that he had already talked to Billy's folks and he would have to miss the games next weekend because that was when the Royals wanted him to come to Surprise. It was now the first of May, and the Royals had already been playing for a month so there would be no Royals there, other than rookies or players recovering from injuries. The "coaches" who would be in charge were minor league coaches and scouts. Billy was floored by this news and didn't even know what to ask Mr. Booker.

Finally, he asked, "Mr. Booker, what are they going to look for?"

"Billy, they already have your stats for the past three years," Mr. Booker started to explain. "They will measure all we've talked about over the years. They obviously want to see how you measure up against others in the five tools we've worked on, including your speed. They will have a minor leaguer pitch to you to see your power, and how much contact you can make against professional pitching. They will want to see you play defense, measuring your range, and your arm. From what I've been told, they want to see if you are as athletic as they've been told by scouts who have followed you the past three years", Mr. Booker added.

Billy was visibly nervous, and Mr. Booker picked up on that immediately.

"Look, Billy, you already have all the tools," said Mr. Booker wanting to encourage the young man. "There is no reason to be nervous. You are 16 years old and have a great future ahead of you, no matter whether the Royals draft you or not", stated the Hall of Fame groundskeeper.

"So how do I get there, Mr. Booker?" Billy asked.

"I will be flying out with you, and will be introducing you to the staff," Mr. Booker answered. "From there, they will tell you what they want you to do, and the rest will be up to you," he finished.

As they arrived at Billy's home, instead of waving goodbye, Mr. Booker asked if he could come in.

Billy's folks were waiting for him because Mr. Booker had already told them the news.

"Dad and Mom, Mr. Booker, said to me you already know about next weekend", Billy sputtered.

"Yes, Billy, we know and are excited for you," his Dad said. "All the work you've done to better yourself has paid off, even if you don't get drafted high this year, but this is fantastic news," Mr. Tankersly told his son.

Billy had told Bobby about his goal, but it was something he hadn't even told his parents. He knew he was going to do his best to impress the Royals that he was worth drafting in the first round.

41

Billy Excels

Billy and Mr. Booker boarded the flight Friday afternoon, as the Royals wanted to see Billy in action Saturday morning. All the way out, Mr. Booker read a book and didn't talk to Billy, other than to answer a couple of questions. Billy wondered how Mr. Booker could be so calm, knowing his "student" for all these years was going to be trying out for the Kansas City Royals. It was almost like he felt no pressure at all for Billy, which seemed to give Billy a little more confidence.

After landing in Phoenix, they went to the hotel, ate dinner and Billy was fast asleep by 9:00 PM. When he woke up around 5:00 AM, he realized he'd been dreaming all night about having a tryout that would make the Royals want to draft him in the first round. He was excited, and not nearly as nervous as he thought he might be. Mr. Booker knocked on his door at 6:00 AM, saying they needed to eat breakfast and get on the way.

Over breakfast, Billy told Mr. Booker about his dream.

"Mr. Booker, I dreamt that I am going to have such a great tryout that the Royals are going to draft me in the first round", he announced to the man who had believed in him for three years now.

"Billy, anything is possible," Mr. Booker told him, encouraging him even more.

As they arrived at the Royals Stadium in Surprise, Mr. Booker introduced him to several of the coaches, and they took it from there.

"Billy, we've been following you ever since Mr. Treehouse first brought your name to us", Loren Gibbons, one of the coaches told him. "We have followed all your stats and had several scouts come to your games over the past three years. As you know, the Amateur draft is taking place next month, and we are making decisions right now on who we hope to draft", explained Coach Gibbons. "We would not have you here today if we were not considering drafting you high, so we want to make sure," he added. "We have already been told that you want to be drafted and will not be going to college, is that correct?" he asked.

"Absolutely, Coach," Billy answered. "I want nothing more than to play professional baseball, eventually reaching the majors," he added.

"That is what we've heard, so today, we are going to be putting you through various drills, measuring you in every way we can," said the Coach. "Go into the clubhouse and get dressed. There will be a uniform for you in there", Coach Gibbons told Billy.

On the way to the clubhouse, Billy saw a figure he recognized. It was George Brett, the Hall of Fame third baseman of the Royals that Billy had read about over and over. There was a statue at Kauffman Stadium in Kansas City that showed him hitting.

"Hi Billy," Mr. Brett said to Billy as they passed. "Good luck today," he told the excited 16-year-old.

As Billy put on his Royals uniform, he wondered if George Brett would be one of the Royals evaluating him today. Then he remembered that he was a vice president of the Royals so there wasn't much doubt that George Brett would be watching him today.

As he walked out to the field, Coach Gibbons said he wanted to see Billy hit against a professional pitcher. He'd brought his own bat with him, and as he stepped into the batter's box, he wondered who was the guy on the mound. He'd never seen him before but figured he was a minor leaguer on a rehab assignment. Billy took the first pitch that he gauged to be in the low 90's, speed-wise. On the next pitch, Billy swung and shattered his bat as he hit a foul ball down the first base line.

"Grab a bat from the dugout," Coach Gibbons instructed. Billy looked over the bats and selected one that said, "Eric Hosmer" on it.

From that moment on, Billy had one of the best days of his life. He hit several balls out of the park, and to each field. He was showing his power in a way that he'd dreamed of the night before. After about 20 minutes of hitting, Coach Gibbons had him take the field, and it was like no matter where they hit it, nothing got by him. His throws to first were on the mark each time, and on the double plays, the second baseman, a minor leaguer by the name of Cat Howsligger, complimented him after several plays. It could not be going better for Billy.

Finally, the Coach wanted to see him run. He timed him to first without hitting, then the same when he batted, and finally, he was asked to drag bunt. Billy knew he impressed everyone at the tryout as several other players stopped what they were doing, and watched Billy.

Then the Coach told him he wanted to see Billy steal second. There was a new pitcher now, and Billy had no idea how fast his pickoff move was. He led off, and immediately dove back to first as the pickoff attempt almost got him. That let him see just how big of a lead he could get, and on the next pitch, Billy broke for second and was safe by a good margin.

"Billy, your speed to first and then your stolen base is as fast as any of our current Royals," Coach Gibbons said to him. This is ending your tryout. So you will know, you lived up to our scouting reports. You can go get dressed now", said the Coach.

Billy walked toward the clubhouse when he saw Mr. Booker talking to George Brett in the grandstands. He wondered what was being said, but right now, he was thrilled with his tryout.

42

Might Get Drafted

On the flight home, all Billy could do was ask Mr. Booker question after question.

"What did George Brett say about my tryout?" Billy asked.

Mr. Booker knew a lot more than he was sharing, but he'd answer Billy's questions with a brief response.

"He said you had a good workout," was Mr. Booker's short answer.

"Do you think the Royals will draft me?" Billy asked.

"Probably," Mr. Booker responded.

The entire flight was like this. Billy asking a question and Mr. Booker giving him a quick and brief answer. By the time they arrived back in KC, Billy had no better idea of where he stood with the Royals than before they left.

Billy's Dad picked them up at the airport and had about as many questions as Billy did, but they were aimed at Billy.

"How did you do, son?" his Dad asked.

"I think I did really well, Dad," responded Billy.

At this point, Mr. Booker opened up.

"Jim, Billy did exceptionally well," he said.

He then told his Dad that everyone he talked to at the camp said Billy would be drafted for sure. The Royals brass felt Billy would go pretty high up in the draft, even if the Royals didn't select him. He went on to say that Billy needed to continue to work on his hitting at the Academy for the three weeks before the draft, but should not play in any games for fear of getting injured. Billy took that as a sign the Royals might draft him, but even he realized that to be drafted in the first round was probably a dream.

When they arrived home, his Mom wanted to know how he did, and Billy answered her the same as he had his Dad. He was tired, and as soon as they had dinner, he excused himself and went to his computer, wanting to check the most recent draft lists. He wasn't surprised to see his name on all the different potential drafts, but he was surprised to see his name listed on one writer's projections as going in the second round. Just then, he heard his Dad say something to his Mom that sounded like, "scouts." He walked to his door and opened it a crack to see if he could overhear their conversation.

"Jim, the scouts, and agents are still calling," he heard his Mom say. "What should we tell Billy?" she asked. Just then, they saw Billy's door open.

"Billy, come on out, Mom and I have something we want to tell you," his Dad said.

"We didn't want to tell you until you got home from your tryout, Billy, but Mom and I have been fielding calls from scouts and agents for the past two months, ever since you graduated," his Dad told his son. "Most wanted to know if you really were going to play pro ball rather than go to college," his Dad continued. "We told them that when you got home from your trip that we were going to suggest you go to Junior College," Mr. Tankersly added.

"Dad," Billy shouted! "Why would you tell them that when you know, I graduated early just so I could be drafted?" Billy screamed.

His parents started laughing, telling him they were joking. Billy knew where he got his "prankster" attitude from.

"Billy, we told them that you graduated early so you would be ready for the draft," his Mom said, smiling at her son. It was still hard for her to think of her 16-year-old son leaving Kansas City to play baseball in the minors some place, but she had grown used to the fact that it was going to happen.

"Son," his Dad said. "Everyone that has called has indicated that you will be drafted high, and we need to start thinking about which agent we want to represent you. There is a short window between the draft, and when you sign, so we have talked to some agents regarding your future", his Dad told Billy.

"We have hired an attorney to represent you after the draft," Billy's Dad continued. "It appears you are going to be drafted high enough that you will be offered a pretty good signing bonus," his Dad explained to him.

"How much, Dad?" Billy asked, not really having any idea. His mind had been on playing the best he could, not on how much money he could make.

"Well, Billy, it depends on which round you are selected," his Dad started explaining. For example, if you get drafted in the 6th round, you will receive a signing bonus of $263,000, but that pretty much has to last until you reach the majors because the pay in the minors is not very much", Mr. Tankersly explained to his son.

"How much do minor leaguers get paid, Dad?" Billy asked.

"If you start in Low A ball, which is probably realistic, you would only receive $1300 a month,

Billy", answered his Dad. "Therefore, and Mom and I are not trying to be negative because we know how much you want to play pro ball, you might start looking at Junior Colleges if you are not drafted high."

"What if I'm drafted higher, Dad?" Billy asked.

"That's the point, Billy," his Mom jumped in. "Because of your age, it is likely that you could be drafted much higher when you are 17, and with a year of Junior College behind you", she continued.

Billy's Dad interrupted his wife saying, "Son, if you waited and happened to go as high as the first round or second round, you would be offered a signing bonus of $1 to $10 million dollars. With an agent, you could be offered more than that, depending on the higher the round and position you are drafted.

"Wow," Billy exclaimed. "I had no idea the difference. I just wanted to play pro ball", he said to his parents. His mind was spinning.

"So, what should I do?" Billy asked, thinking for the first time that maybe he should go to Junior College for a year.

"Well, first things first, Billy," said his Dad. "We have to wait until the draft, which is June 7th to see how high you are drafted. Should you be drafted as high as the second round, we have advised Pete Browwser, the agent for many of the Royals, that we would like for him to represent you. He's agreed, but only if you are selected by the second round.

43

Draft Day

The days passed slowly for Billy while waiting for the draft. After his tryout for the Royals, he felt that he realistically could be drafted by the Royals as high as the second round, but as draft day neared, he felt more and more like he needed to think about Junior College. He went to the Academy every day, hitting from the cages until he had blisters. He knew someday, he would be playing major league baseball, but after his folks had explained the little money that minor leaguers made, he felt he almost had to be drafted high, or consider Junior College.

The draft was going to be on ESPN. Billy could hardly wait. Finally, June 7th arrived. Billy, Mr. Booker, Coach Heier and his parents were all glued to the TV set in the Tankersly's living room. The Minnesota Twins had the first pick, and they selected Salvador Escobar, a kid from Houston who played 1B. Billy had not heard Bobby ever talk about him, but the announcers said that Salvador would be receiving a minimum signing bonus of $6,125,000 for being the number one pick. They added that his agent was Arnie Hart, which meant he could expect to receive a great deal more.

Billy heard that number and thought, "Maybe I should wait a year before signing, no matter how high I am drafted."

Cincinnati had the second pick, and they selected Carter Gurney, an outfielder from the University of Texas. It was announced that as the second pick, he would also receive a minimum signing bonus of $6,125,000. By now, Billy was pretty sure he might be going to Junior College.

The announcers explained that the first five picks would all receive the same minimum, and then it dropped down; the further a player was from the top, in each round. All players in the first round would make a minimum of $1,851,000, and players in the second round, a minimum of $1,064,000. Again, the announcers talked about the player's agents, and how much money could be added to the minimum.

Billy decided that next year, after one year of Junior College, he would get an agent, no matter what round he was selected. The first five players selected were from the south, and Billy was thinking, "Maybe I could go to a Junior College in Austin, and play with Bobby for a year."

As each player was selected, Billy realized that most had played down south or had gone to college. He had played against many of the players being drafted on the trips to Austin and Phoenix. Billy knew the Royals drafted last in the first round but didn't know when they drafted in the second round.

"Mr. Booker, do you know when the Royals draft in the second round?" Billy asked.

"Through a trade they made, Billy, they will be drafting 5th in the second round", Mr. Booker replied.

Billy's heart sank. He was hoping they might draft him if they were last in the second round, but not if they drafted that high.

"What about the third round, Mr. Booker?" he asked.

"They don't draft until 15th in the third round, Billy", Mr. Booker said.

"How much do players sign for in the 3rd round?" Billy asked.

"$632,000, Billy, but you have to understand, that money has to last a kid until he reaches the majors because of the pay in the minors, even in Triple-A, is only $2100 a month", explained Mr. Booker. He went on to say, "Billy, this is why you might want to wait a year before signing if you are selected in the third round or later."

Billy finally understood what his folks had tried to explain to him, and why they suggested he look at Junior Colleges. So far, out of the first 20 players selected, only one had come from a team or school in the north.

For the next hour, eleven more players were selected, and Billy had played against at least four of them in Austin and another three in Phoenix. But all were from the south, or college graduates. His hopes were dwindling. As the announcers made a point to explain how much each player was receiving as a signing bonus, and comparing it to players selected in later rounds, Billy was already thinking about playing baseball with Bobby again. He knew, with another year's experience, he might be drafted in the first or second round. Everyone had been correct; his age was going to work against him.

He was getting more and more discouraged, as some of the teams who had already drafted, had talked to Billy over the past year or two. But each selected a player from the south.

After another 15 minutes or so, the Royals were next on the clock. By now, Billy figured, at best, he would be selected in the second round, which didn't start until the next day. He sat glued to the TV to see if the Royals picked a shortstop. That would almost assure that he would not be selected in the second or third round.

Before the Royals selection, ESPN cut away to a commercial. They always did that. When the ESPN announcers came back on, they talked for a bit about the last selection, and then predicted that Aaron Towns, a shortstop, would be selected by the Royals.

"Towns has good size, and speed. He stole 42 bases for Nathan High, in Houston", the announcer reported. "He fits right into the Royals format and will be a good fit for them," the second announcer replied.

Billy remembered playing against Aaron in Austin. He knew Towns was a good player. The announcers had been pretty much on the mark all afternoon with each selection, so Billy started thinking about "what if another team selected him in the second round?" He wanted to play for the Royals, but more importantly, he just wanted to play.

"Mr. Booker, do you know where the Astro's pick in the second round?" Billy asked, thinking playing for the Astro's would be cool since Billy lived close to Houston. His mind was whirling around the fact that the Royals were going to select Towns, and would definitely not select two shortstops in the first two rounds.

Billy watched the commissioner of baseball walk to the podium, with the Royals selection. He paused, took a deep breath and announced:

"With the last pick of the first round, the World Series Champion Kansas City Royals, have selected a homegrown speedster from the Leawood Baseball Academy, Billy Tankersly

"What?" Billy was stunned. "Had he actually heard that?" he thought. As the announcers started talking about him, explaining that he was the youngest in the history of baseball to be drafted in the first round, he realized he'd heard them correctly.

He started jumping up and down, screaming, "I'm going to be playing professional baseball" His parents, Mr. Booker and Coach Heier were screaming with Billy, shouting their congratulations.

All of his hard work had paid off. Billy Tankersly's first dream had just come true.

Billy heard his Skype ringing, and before anyone could stop him, he was talking to Bobby.

"Billy, you did it," Bobby shouted. "I thought you were so unrealistic when you told me your goal. You did it. A first round pick. Wow, Billy. That is fantastic", Bobby's words came out faster than Billy's thoughts.

Finally, Billy got to talk.

"Bobby, this was only my first goal. Remember what I told you back on the Rockets?"

"Sure, you've told me enough times," answered Bobby. "You are going to set the major league record for stolen bases because you can wear metal spikes," Bobby laughed.

"It may take me four years to reach the majors, but I'll only be 20. Ricky Henderson, who has the record of 1406 stolen bases, was 20 when he reached the major leagues", Billy ran the numbers by Bobby like he knew all this information, because, in Billy's mind, 1406 was a number everyone should know.

"I think you will do it, Billy," said Bobby with almost as much confidence as the new Kansas City Royals draftee.

Billy remembered the clang of his spikes that first day, hitting the pavement in the parking lot, running to the water fountain to see Bobby, only to be told he could not wear metal spikes in Little League. Now, he hoped he would hear that clang for many years to come.

-The End-

On the next page find the first two chapters of the next book in the **Metal Spikes Series**.

Metal Spikes II

1

Arriving at the Class A Lexington Legends ballpark, his metal spikes hanging from his shoulders, Billy was ready to start his professional career.

The Legends had already begun their season, so the pressure was on Billy to adjust quickly to get in the starting lineup.

"Hey Rookie," one of the players yelled as Billy walked into the clubhouse. Billy wasn't sure if he was being razzed or the player was friendly. He found out real fast.

"Come over here and shine my spikes," the young player directed Billy.

"Hi, I'm Billy Tankersly," he said as he held his hand out for a handshake.

"I don't think you heard me, rookie.....I need my spikes shined", commanded this apparent bully. Billy wondered if this kid, not much older than him, knew he was talking to a first round pick? Then he thought back to a conversation with this Dad about not getting too cocky and thinking too much of himself.

"What's your name?" Billy asked, ignoring the shoe shine remark.

"Leve Peterson," he answered.

"What position do you play?" Billy asked.

"Left Field, Billy," he responded, holding his hand out to Billy.

They shook hands, and Leve told Billy he was just kidding about the shoeshine, but rookies had to have some sort of experience to start their professional baseball career. Billy laughed, sort of a nervous laugh.

Billy was surprised the Royals had started him here in Lexington instead of the Rookie League, where most newly drafted players started.

Leve had been signed last year, and this was a promotion for him because he started in the Rookie League last year. As the other players showed up, Leve introduced each of them to Billy, and before he knew it, he was dressed in his Legends uniform and on the field ready to take batting practice.

It was three hours before game time, and Billy was amazed to see how much preparation went into each game–even at the minor league level When it was his turn to take batting practice, the Manager, Vern Wanamaker, came over to talk to Billy.

"Billy, we are really glad to have you here," he started. Pedro Reddington, our shortstop, got injured last week, and we've been short-handed ever since. You think you could start today's game?" the coach quizzed Billy.

The 16-year old didn't even blink as he answered, "Absolutely." His confidence level was at an all-time high, ever since his name was announced as the Royals first round pick in the draft.

He stepped into the batting cage and immediately let three pitches go by without swinging. He was waiting for his pitch.

"Billy, do you know what contact hitting is?" the coach said as Billy stepped back away from the plate before the next pitch.

"That's the way the Royals play," answered Billy.

"Yes it is, and it's the way we train here at the Legends," drawled Coach Wanamaker, who obviously was from the south.

"I want you to hit the next pitch, wherever it is pitched," instructed Billy's first professional coach.

The next pitch was outside, but Billy hit a line drive to left field that rolled into the gap.

"That's what I'm talking about, Billy," the coach yelled, praising Billy.

"The Royals complete minor league system has to learn to hit this way, Billy, because when we make contact, even if we don't hit it hard, it gives us more of a chance to get on base and score runs," Coach Wanamaker explained. "Many major league teams have adopted our way of playing after the Royals won the World Series last year."

"I've always been taught to wait for my pitch," Billy explained to the Coach.

"Yes, Billy, but you are now a professional, and you are going to have to learn to do things differently than you did as an amateur," Coach Wanamaker said.

Billy remembered Mr. Booker telling him that he had to respect authority, and really listen and learn as coaches tried to teach him. He realized, "This is what Mr. Booker meant", as he hit one ball after another from the cage. No matter where the pitch was unless it was so far from him that he could not make contact, he was swinging....and having fun doing it.

2

The game started with nearly 2000 fans in the stands. Billy was starting, hitting 8th, something he'd never done.

The Legend's trailed, 2-0, in the 3rd inning when Billy finally got up. Like he'd trained himself to do, he had been watching the West Virginia pitcher like a hawk. The West Virginia Power led the South Atlantic League's Northern Division with a 20-10 record while the Legends, in the South Division, were crawling along with an 11-19 record.

The pitcher for the Power was Oscar Bratwich, who Billy was going to face in his first professional at-bat. Before stepping into the batter's box, he stopped, looked around the field and over to the dugout. This was a memory he wanted to keep forever.

Bratwich started Billy with a curve that broke inside, and Billy let it go for Ball One. He wondered if Coach Wanamaker would have had him swing at that pitch.

The next pitch was a fastball, right over the heart of the plate. Billy saw the ball hit his bat before it darted in the gap between center field and right field. Billy started for second but put the brakes on as the right fielder gobbled it up and had it back to second faster than any outfielder he'd ever seen.

"My first professional hit," thought Billy, his heart pounding as he looked to see the signs from the 3rd base coach, Coach Neil, hoping they knew he could steal. The Legend players in the dugout were all cheering for Billy, because of rookie or not; they wanted to win.

Billy saw the steal sign as Mack Monroe; the second baseman stepped into the box. Mack was a second year player on the Legends, like Leve, and knew to take the first pitch, giving Billy the chance to steal.

He had been watching Bratwich on every pitch, but the only two hits for the Legends, other than Billy's, were doubles, so Billy didn't get to study his pickoff move.

He took a decent size lead, but one where he knew he could get back safely if Bratwich tried to pick him off. Sure enough, over to first base came a pickoff throw. Billy didn't even bother to dive back. He knew it was Bratwich's warning pickoff, not a real pickoff....and there was a difference as he'd learned last year with the Yankees.

Billy took a bigger lead, and before he knew it, Bratwich was throwing to first again. Billy dove, stretching his arm, hand, and fingers to tag the bag before he got tagged.

"Safe," yelled the ump.

Billy had never seen a pickoff move that fast...and sneaky. He didn't hesitate, though, once he saw Bratwich's leg cross the mound on his first pitch to Mack. He was headed to second.

"Safe" yelled the ump, as Billy slid in head first.

Billy had his first professional stolen base. He had already looked up the single-season stolen base record for the Legends and was shocked to find that it belonged to Delino Hopkins, who was in Triple-A this year. Billy had read about Hopkins in the Kansas City Star because he was touted as a future Royal.

"OK, only 82 more bases to steal this year", thought Billy, completely forgetting that only 40 games were remaining for the Legends.

On the next pitch, Mack hit a slow dribbler to 3rd base. The third basemen didn't even bother to look at Billy assuming he'd stay at second base. By the time he picked it up and threw casually to first, Billy was rounding third, on his way to the plate.

The first baseman caught the ball as a routine catch, looking back to second to make sure Billy was still there. By the time he realized Billy was on his way to the plate, his throw was hurried and on the first base side, allowing Billy to slide in safely.

As the ump yelled, "Safe," Billy's new teammates were out of the dugout and giving Billy chest bumps.

That was the spark the Legends needed, and they came back to win 5-3. Billy ended his first professional game with one hit, a walk, and one stolen base. He scored both times he was on base.

It seemed strange to Billy to play a full 9-inning game, but the feeling after a win was good, no matter how many innings they played. With all the excitement in the clubhouse, there was no one more excited than Billy Tankersly. He was a professional ball player with a stolen base in his first game.

As he sat by his locker, while changing clothes, he could hardly wait to get back to his temporary living quarters, a hotel on Lexington Street. He just hoped they had WiFi so he could Skype his best friend, Bobby Banks in Austin, Texas, to tell him about his first professional game.

"Hey Bobby, guess what?" Billy started, as soon as he got to his room.

"I don't have to guess, Billy," he declared. "I found the Lexington radio station and listened. Congratulations, Mr. Stolen Base King",

Look for Metal Spikes II on July 1, 2017

What is your Dream?

We all have dreams. Some dreams seem impractical. We forget them almost as soon as they come into our mind. In Metal Spikes, Billy's dream seemed impractical and impossible to Bobby. But, Billy believed he could achieve it. He did things to make his dream come true. What is your dream? Decide what you would really like in your life. The power to make it happen is already within you.

Billy had a dream. He was determined to make it come true, no matter what he had to sacrifice. Reaching dreams means sacrificing something, like Billy having to mow yards instead of playing video games. Are you willing to do something that you would rather not do, in order to achieve what you want? That is what it means to sacrifice.

Billy set goals. He visualized his dream coming true, over and over. He practiced harder and longer than others. Have you set goals and visualized your dreams coming true? They can. It's up to you.

To reach his dream, Billy learned he must have a burning desire. That meant telling others about his dream. Others will then keep reminding you like Bobby did with Billy. It will keep your goal in front of you, helping build the faith necessary for you to move forward. Once you have a goal, you must spend time thinking about it every day and taking action steps toward attaining it.

Billy learned that repetition is what helps build faith. He constantly reminded himself of Ricky Henderson's stolen base mark. He practiced the things necessary to break that mark, enabling him to believe it was possible, even when others could not see it. Picture in your mind that you have already reached your goal. You must "see it" before it can come true.

Billy learned to encourage other players at the very first team meeting with the Rockets. Coach Yam taught the team not to belittle or criticize the other players if they messed up, but to encourage and praise each other. It was called Team Spirit. Have you encouraged someone today...your brother/sister or parents? Try telling them how much you appreciate them. Watch their reaction.

He learned the value of listening intently, not just on the ball field but in the classroom. He was able to get his grades up by really focusing on what the teacher was saying. Listening intently to the other person lets you learn about that person, and causes them to look up to you because you are showing them sincere appreciation by listening.

He learned disappointment happens when Coach Yam told him he could not wear Metal Spikes in Little League, and when he ended up in the hospital with knee damage. He learned to pray and ask God for what he needed. When in the hospital, he believed his dream was being answered, and he had a thankful heart.

Billy learned that disappointment can turn into an opportunity. He realized the secret was, "Don't quit". Keep your goal in mind as often as possible because when one door closes, another opens. Opportunity comes in many ways. All of us, adults and kids, meet disappointment but the ones who keep a good attitude eventually outrun the disappointment, and find another opportunity.

Billy thought many things adults said didn't make sense. As Billy got more experience and started listening intently to what he was being told, it ended up making absolute sense. This was the one thing that helped Billy mature enough to be drafted. No matter how old we are, we can always learn from others who have more experience than us.

About the Author

Warren Haskin grew up on the outskirts of Kansas City in Mission, Kansas. When he became a Cub Scout, his Dad and several other fathers obtained land at the edge of town to build a baseball diamond for their sons. From that moment on, Warren was determined to be the best baseball player ever.

He played college baseball in the Big 12 for the University of Kansas Jayhawks and for the Navy in a semi-pro league in Memphis, Tennessee. As ayoung husband and father of two, he embarked on a life-long career as an entrepreneur developing programs using much of what he'd learned from baseball.

Warren's passion for the sport has remained throughout his life. He has been a player, coach, sports editor, baseball and football announcer, business developer and owner, and trainer.

This is Warren's first fiction book. His inspirational teaching shows from the first to the last chapter through "coaches", along the way, who teach young people and adults how to succeed.

He currently resides in Austin, Texas and is a business and personal consultant for Help People, Inc. He can be reached at whaskin@HelpPeople.com.

www.ingramcontent.com/pod-product-compliance
Lightning Source LLC
LaVergne TN
LVHW010055110826
845155LV00028B/349

* 9 7 8 1 9 4 4 0 7 1 2 4 0 *